CAMBRIDGE LIBRARY COLLECTION

Books of enduring scholarly value

British and Irish History, Nineteenth Century

This series comprises contemporary or near-contemporary accounts of the political, economic and social history of the British Isles during the nineteenth century. It includes material on international diplomacy and trade, labour relations and the women's movement, developments in education and social welfare, religious emancipation, the justice system, and special events including the Great Exhibition of 1851.

Dactylography and The Origin of Finger-Printing

The Scottish doctor Henry Faulds (1843–1930) and the English judge Sir William James Herschel (1833–1917) both recognised the potential of fingerprints as a means of identification. While working in Japan, Faulds had developed his methods after noticing impressions on ancient pottery. Herschel, during his service as a magistrate in India, had introduced a system of using fingerprints as a way of preventing fraud. In the course of a lengthy controversy, Faulds sought to be acknowledged for the significance of his discoveries. Although there is no doubt that Faulds was first to publish on the subject, it was Herschel's work, begun in the 1850s, which was later developed by Galton and Henry as the tool of forensic science we know today. Reissued here together, these two works, first published in 1912 and 1916 respectively, are Faulds' overview of the subject and Herschel's account of his work in India.

T0371466

Cambridge University Press has long been a pioneer in the reissuing of out-of-print titles from its own backlist, producing digital reprints of books that are still sought after by scholars and students but could not be reprinted economically using traditional technology. The Cambridge Library Collection extends this activity to a wider range of books which are still of importance to researchers and professionals, either for the source material they contain, or as landmarks in the history of their academic discipline.

Drawing from the world-renowned collections in the Cambridge University Library and other partner libraries, and guided by the advice of experts in each subject area, Cambridge University Press is using state-of-the-art scanning machines in its own Printing House to capture the content of each book selected for inclusion. The files are processed to give a consistently clear, crisp image, and the books finished to the high quality standard for which the Press is recognised around the world. The latest print-on-demand technology ensures that the books will remain available indefinitely, and that orders for single or multiple copies can quickly be supplied.

The Cambridge Library Collection brings back to life books of enduring scholarly value (including out-of-copyright works originally issued by other publishers) across a wide range of disciplines in the humanities and social sciences and in science and technology.

Dactylography and The Origin of Finger-Printing

Henry Faulds
William J. Herschel

Cambridge
University Press

CAMBRIDGE
UNIVERSITY PRESS

University Printing House, Cambridge, CB2 8BS, United Kingdom

Cambridge University Press is part of the University of Cambridge.
It furthers the University's mission by disseminating knowledge in the pursuit of education, learning and research at the highest international levels of excellence.

www.cambridge.org
Information on this title: www.cambridge.org/9781108081252

This edition first published 1912–16
This digitally printed version 2015

ISBN 978-1-108-08125-2 Paperback

Dactylography

Or, THE STUDY OF FINGER-PRINTS

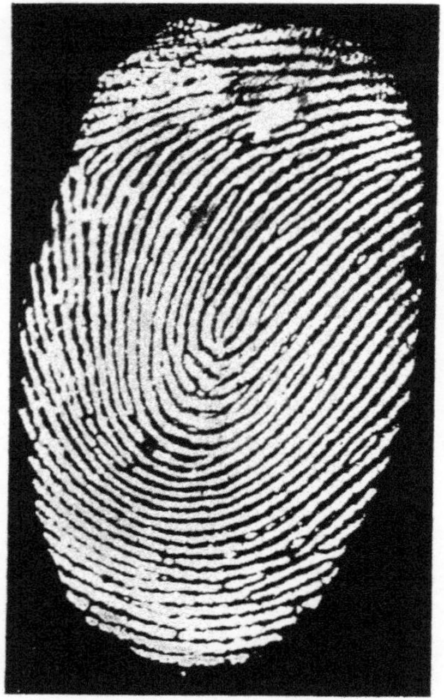

GREASY SMUDGE
(Vivified by white powder).

ACCIDENTAL SMUDGE
(encircled for presentation).

A "NEGATIVE" THUMB-PRINT,
furrows and pores black, ridges white.

Dactylography, frontispiece]

DACTYLOGRAPHY

OR

THE STUDY OF FINGER-PRINTS

BY

HENRY FAULDS

L.R.F.P. & S. F.R. ANTHROP. INST.,
M.R. ARCHÆOL. INST. M. SOCIOL. SOC.

Illustrated

HALIFAX
MILNER & COMPANY
RAGLAN WORKS

CONTENTS.

LIST OF ILLUSTRATIONS

Dactylography

OR THE STUDY OF FINGER-PRINTS

CHAPTER I

INTRODUCTION : EARLY HINTS AND RECENT PROGRESS

DACTYLOGRAPHY deals with what is of scientific interest and practical value in regard to the lineations in the skin on the fingers and toes, or rather on the hands and feet of men, monkeys, and allied tribes, which lineations form patterns of great variety and persistence. The Greeks used the term δάκτυλος τοῦ ποδός (*daktylos tou podos*, finger of the foot) for a toe ; and the toes are of almost as much interest to the dactylographer as the fingers, and present similar patterns for study.

In primitive times the savage hunter had to use all his wits sharply in the examination of foot and toe marks, whether of the game he pursued or the human foe he guarded against, and he learned to deduce many a curious lesson with Sherlock Holmes-like acuteness and precision. The recency, the rate of motion, the length of stride, the degree of fatigue, the number, and kinds and conditions of men or beasts that had impressed their traces on the soil, all could be read by him with ease and promptness. Such imprints have been preserved in early Mexican picture writings.

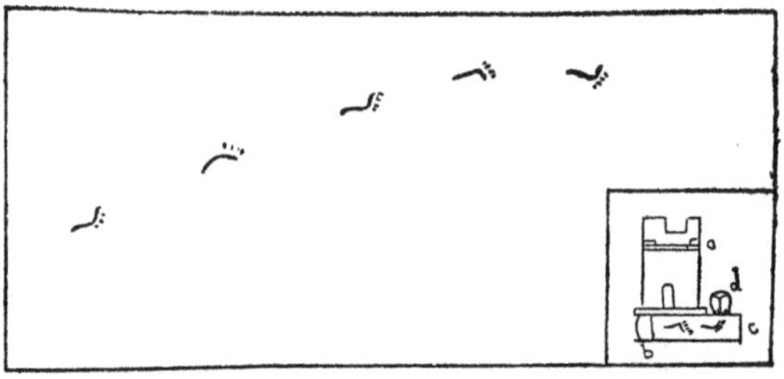

FOOTPRINTS IN ANCIENT MEXICAN REMAINS.
Inset: Threshold with Foot-Marks (also Mexican).

In a similar way the palæontologist strives to interpret the impress made by organisms on primeval mud flats or sandy shores æons ago. There are numbers, whole species indeed, of extinct jelly fishes the existence of which has never been known directly, but that there once were such beings in the world has been confidently deduced from the permanent impressions their soft and perishable bodies have left in the fine texture of certain rocks. The Chinese tell us that one of their sages first learned to write and to teach the use of written characters by observing the marks made by a bird's claws.

When we approach the limits of written history we begin to hear faint inarticulate murmurs of a time when the lines on human fingers began to arrest notice and interest. Thus we sometimes find in later neolithic pottery, nail and finger marks, used to adorn the sun-dried pots in common use. The Babylonians used their finger nails as seal-marks on commercial tablets, and the Chinese have occasionally done the same. Not many years ago, as I myself have often witnessed, when sealing-wax or wafers were used more than they are now, servant girls were wont to impress their thumb-mark on the soft wafer or wax. There are several characters in the Chinese alphabet (of some 30,000 letters) which suggest such a use of finger-marks as seals, but after many years' enquiry, I have not yet seen any direct evidence of their use for such a purpose.* The term *Sho-seki* is used in Japanese to denote foot-prints, and also the tracking of anyone. I have not met any passage or expression in which finger-prints are mentioned in Japanese works, except in regard to fantastical images of footprints of Buddha and the like. It is claimed, however, that prisoners on conviction were required to adhibit their mark as a seal of confession.† There has been no evidence adduced that either in China or Japan was there ever a system of identification by that means, although it is conceivable that the form of making a sign-manual may have originated from some dim perception of their value for identification.

In a similar way finger-marks were used, as I have been informed, in India, even before the mutiny, and were supposed to be used like the cross made by illiterate people in this country. The numerals up to five seem to have been obtained by marking off fingers. A dactylic origin of V as an open hand, complete with outstretched thumb, has been favoured. X (ten) might easily then be obtained by placing two V's apex to apex.

There are certain folds or creases in palms and soles, which are formed very much as the creases in gloves or boots are formed, and with those the dactylographer is

*In Professor Giles's *Chinese-English Dictionary* (1909) on page 223 some characters are given for "to make a finger-print," etc.

†See *Nature* (January 17th, 1895), "Finger-Print Method," Kumagusa Minakata.

not much concerned. Such lines were supposed by many to mark the fateful influence of stars on the destiny of their owner, and are the basis of palmistry. Similar lines are found in apes. There are general patterns of lineations all over the palmar surface of the hands and the plantar surface of the feet which are of some interest, but the chief practical concern of most students in this new field is with certain points where patterns run into forms of great complexity, especially in the palmar skin covering the last joint of each finger. It is not common to find either in pots or pictures those patterns printed clearly, but the creases dear to the palmister are frequently enough shown.

In Mr. C. Ainsworth Mitchell's *Science and the Criminal*, published in 1911, a case is mentioned of a very early finger-print, if the evidence has not been fallacious :—

> "In the prehistoric flint-holes at Brandon, in Suffolk, there was found some years ago a pick made from the horn of an extinct elk. This had been used by some flint-digger of the Stone Age to hew out of the chalk the rough flints which were subsequently made into scrapers and arrow-heads. Upon the dark handle of this instrument were the finger-prints in chalk of the workman, who, thousands of years ago, flung it down for the last time."

It is now in the British Museum. A foot-print also has been found of very early date.

Such white marks on a dark ground are often very clear, showing the detail of lineations well, and presuming, as is natural, that the ordinary precautions were taken to secure that they were not recent accidental additions to the remains, such a record is highly valuable.

It was apparently a common practice in ancient India to adorn buildings with crude finger-marks made with white or red sandal-wood. The red hand common on door-posts and the like in Arabia does not usually show any lineations, but in some few ancient and primitive carvings and in sun-baked pot-work, patterns occur which appear to me to have probably had finger-print lineations as a *motif*. Professor Sollas, in writing of Palæolithic Races in *Science Progress* (April, 1909)—a subject of which he is a master—says: "Impressions of the human hand are met with painted in red in Altamira, but in other caves also in black, and sometimes uncoloured on a coloured ground. These seem to be older than any of the other markings." Some cases are stencilled, as with Australians to-day.

The same writer, in a foot-note, also states, in describing caves and paintings of modern Bushmen: "Impressions of the human hand are also met with on the walls of these caves."

A traveller, Mr. John Bradbury, who witnessed the return of a war-party of the Aricara Indians, says:—

> "Many of them had the mark which indicates that they had drank the blood of an enemy. This mark is made by rubbing the hand all over with vermilion, and by laying it on the mouth it leaves a complete impression on the face, which is designed to resemble and indicate a bloody hand."—[*Travels in the Interior of America* (1817).]

The ancient bloody hand of Ulster is well known, and other examples occur which might be quoted.

Some "prehistoric pottery" was found last autumn at Avebury, North Wilts, of which I have not seen full particulars. In a press paragraph, however, it is stated that its chief interest "centres in the fact that it is ornamented on both faces—the impressions of twisted grass (or cord) and finger-nails being clearly defined." It is temporarily classified as a type of pottery associated with long barrows and neolithic pits.

My own attention was first directed to the patterns in finger-prints, as they occurred impressed on sun-baked pottery which I found in the numerous shell-heaps dotted around the great Bay of Yedo. The subject was quite unknown to me till then, in the seventies. No pottery has yet been found which belongs to the early stone stage of man's culture. But with evidence of the use of fire, and of the manufacture of polished stone weapons, fragments of rude hand-moulded pottery—sun-baked or fire-burned—begin to be associated. Sometimes these are quite clearly seen to be moulded with the aid of human fingers, the nails only making a clear mark, but in other cases the finger furrows are prominently indented in regular patterns, which cannot, I think, be distinguished from those made by men of our own race and time. In the formal Japanese ceremony of social tea-drinking, or *Cha-no-yu*, pottery of this Archaic kind, with finger patterns indented in the clay, is highly esteemed. In an article on this kind of pottery by Mr. Charles Holme, in *The Studio* (February, 1909), one example is described thus: "It is modelled in a brown clay entirely by hand, without the aid of a potter's wheel. The impressions of the fingers made in shaping the bowl are carefully retained," etc. Not till Celtic times in Europe is there evidence of the use of the potter's wheel.

I am surprised to find how very little attention has

yet been given to finger imprints on early pottery. My own opportunities for observation have in late years been severely limited, but I have seldom had a peep at ancient potsherds without discovering some few traces of the kind of impressions, accidental or designed, which I have described. I have not had early Teutonic pottery specially under observation, but Professor G. Baldwin Brown, who is an accomplished authority in that department, wrote me thus :—

> "In the early Teutonic pottery, so far as I have examined it, the ornamental patterns are produced by drawing lines and furrows with some hard tool, such as a shaped point of wood or bone. It is very rarely that the furrows or circular depressions have the soft edges which would suggest the use of the finger, and I have never noticed the texture of the finger-tip impressed on the clay, though I have not looked specially for this with a glass. Ornaments are also commonly impressed with a wooden stamp on which some simple pattern has been cut. The only ornamental motive which seems to spring directly out of manipulation by the fingers is the projecting boss, characteristic of a certain class of Teutonic ware. The clay is forced out from within in the form of a knob or a flute, and the idea of such an ornamental treatment has probably arisen from the accidental projections produced in the exterior surface of the vase by the pressure of the fingers when the vase is being shaped from within. There is nothing in early Teutonic pottery like the coiled Pueblo pots, or other products where the pressure of the fingers on the exterior has generated the whole ornamental scheme."

Antique references to finger-print patterns are not numerous. In the anatomical text-books of my student days, I cannot recall a single example of their having been noticed or figured, and no figure was printed in the usual plates of anatomy of my time. Malpighi, writing in 1686, tersely alludes to the ridges which, he says, form different patterns (*diversas figuras describunt*).

Both Sir William Herschel and myself have publicly called for evidence of the alleged use in the Far East of finger-prints being used for identification. During my residence in Japan I was intimate with the leading antiquarians, and was repeatedly assured that nothing was known by them of any such legal process. Mr. T. W. Rhys Davids, Secretary of the Royal Asiatic Society, of which I was formerly a member, wrote me in answer to an inquiry as to this point, on the 17th May, 1905 :—

> " DEAR SIR,—I have heard of thumb marks being used in the East as sign-manuals, but I know no single case of thumb or finger marks being used for identification, and, pending further information, I do not believe they ever were so used in ancient times in any part of the East."

Every now and again I receive letters telling me of some one who thinks he remembers some one saying that he saw, etc., etc. Now, surely, it would not be difficult if anyone were to find such evidence, to send a copy or photograph duly authenticated, and a date attested subsequent to the date of publication by *Nature*, in 1880, of the correspondence on this subject. A good deal has been written about Professor J. E. Purkenje (or Purkinje) in this connection. One enthusiastic fellow-countryman has mentioned with eulogy a purely imaginary course of lectures on Identification by Finger-Prints. Purkinje does not seem ever to have dreamed of putting them to such a use. In *The Daily News* of January 23rd, 1911, an interview is reported with Sir Edward Henry, who is made to state that

Purkinje "wrote about the value of finger-prints for purposes of identification"; but on enquiry Sir Edward assured me he had not said anything beyond what was stated in his work on Finger-Prints, and in that work, of course, no such statement is hinted at as that Purkinje proposed to secure identification by finger-prints.

As a student I was fairly well acquainted with much of what that keen observer had written, and when I was lecturing to medical students in Japan on the Testimony of the Senses, I could not help noticing that while Purkinje had been busy with the fingers and with the special development in their sensitive tips of the organs of touch, no records had been preserved which mentioned his notice of the finger-furrows or the patterns made by them. I took much trouble in the matter, writing to eminent authorities and to librarians, and found no trace of any such work. Sir F. Galton, in his published writings, is quite in accord with me so far, but he has not explained how he came to think of Purkinje's work. Writing in 1892 on *Finger-Prints*, (p. 85) he says of the subsequent discovery of a thesis of 58 pages: "No copy of the pamphlet existed in any public medical library in England, nor in any private one, so far as I could learn; neither could I get a sight of it at some important Continental libraries. One copy was known of it in America." The American copy was not known generally till I had made vigorous enquiries there. Sir F. Galton adds, "The very zealous librarian of the Royal College of Surgeons was so good as to take much pains at my instance to procure one: his zeal was happily and unexpectedly rewarded by success, and the copy is now securely lodged in the library of the college."

As Sir Francis began to give attention to this subject in 1888 (p. 2 of work just quoted) it is only justice to myself in the matter to state that in June, 1886, I called on the then librarian of the Royal College and impressed upon him my conviction that as nothing had then been known of any printed work by Purkinje on this topic, a search among his remaining papers should be made, as to me it seemed improbable that, working so closely in that field, Purkinje could fail to observe the patterns of the finger-furrows. It seemed as certain a deduction to me as was that of the existence of Neptune before that planet had been actually discovered. The pamphlet is in Latin, a work of 58 pages, printed at Vratislav, (i.e., Breslau) in 1823. In the article on "Finger-Prints," in the *Encyclopædia Britannica* (1911) it is stated that "the permanent character of the finger-print was put forward scientifically in 1823 by J. E. Purkinje, an eminent professor of physiology, who read a paper before the university of Breslau," etc. But he was surely not a professor when graduating, and what passage in that thesis, may I ask, deals scientifically with the *permanent character* of the finger-print? Purkinje had studied the lineations of monkeys as well as those of men.

In *Tristram Shandy* (1765) we read of "the marks of a snuffy finger and thumb."

Jack Shepherd, a novel of Ainsworth's, was published in 1839. One Van Galgebrook, a Dutch conjuror, therein foretells Jack's bad end: "From a black mole under the child's right ear, shaped like a coffin . . . and a deep line just above the middle of the left thumb, meeting round about in the form of a noose." It would be interesting to know how Ainsworth happened upon the suggestion.

Bewick sometimes jestingly left his sign-mark on his fine wood-engravings, and those thus attested by his thumb-print are now specially valued.

Many references occur in modern literature to finger-prints, and in *David Copperfield*, published in complete form in 1850, Charles Dickens tells how Dan'l Peggotty, in the old boat-house at Yarmouth, "printed off fishy impressions of his thumb on all the cards he found."

SINGLE FINGER-PRINT

Pater, in 1871, writing of the Poetry of Michelangelo, mentions "the little seal of red wax which the stranger entering Bologna must carry on the thumb of his right hand."

Later references are very common after the eighties. Alix in 1867–8 wrote on the papillary lines of hand and foot in *Zoologie*, vols. viii. and ix., contributions which were first brought to my notice after the publication of my *Guide*.

In 1879 I engaged a Japanese engraver in Tokyo to make for me copperplate forms in which to receive impressions of the fingers of both hands in their consecutive or serial order. There were spaces for information to be recorded which might be useful in anthropology, and a place to which a lock of hair of the subject was to be attached. The original proof sheet, marked by me in red pencil where special points in the rugæ were to be carefully printed, is now in the library of The Royal Faculty of Physicians and Surgeons in Glasgow, along with a letter to me from Charles Darwin on the subject

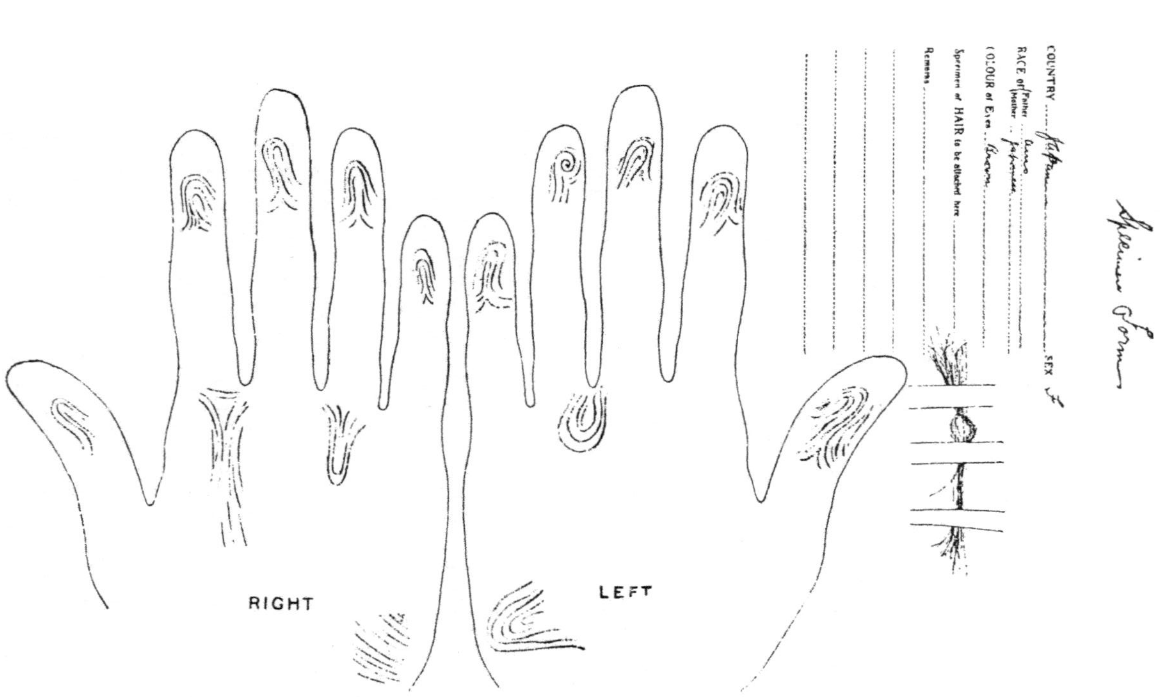

FACSIMILE (REDUCED) OF THE ORIGINAL OUTLINE FORMS FOR BOTH HANDS.
Done in copperplate for the author in Japan at close of 1879 or in January, 1880. The lineations were filled in with pencil at the same period.

of finger-prints. The figures are from reduced photographs of those two original copperplate forms, which have never before been published except as accompanying the circular mentioned below. Many of those forms were sent to travellers and residents in foreign countries, with a written circular, as follows :—

"January, 1880.

"Dear Sir,

"I am at present engaged in a comparative study of the *rugæ*, or skin-furrows, of the hands of different races, and would esteem it as a great favour if you should obtain for me nature-prints from the palmar surface of the fingers of any of the ....race in your vicinity, in accordance with the enclosed forms. The points of special interest are marked [with red crosses] and no others need specially be attended to. Each point must be printed by itself separately. Printer's ink put on very thinly and evenly, so as not to obliterate the furrows of the skin, is best. It can easily be removed by benzine or turpentine. In place of that, burnt cork mixed with *very little* oil will do very well. One or two trials had better be made before printing on the forms. If printing should be found too difficult, sketches of leading lines—at the points indicated—would still be of very great value, taking care that the directions corresponded with the furrows, and not in *reverse*, as when a simple impression is taken. If any one finger, and so on, comes out badly, a piece of paper can be printed and pasted on at the proper place. I enclose as a specimen a filled-up form. [The fingers printed in the proper spaces and the important 'points' each marked with a cross in red pencil.]

"As novel and valuable ethnological results are expected from this enquiry, I trust this may form a sufficient excuse for asking you to take so much trouble. Please return any forms which may be filled up to the above address.

"I am, etc.,

"Henry Faulds."

Many of these circulars were posted with great care to recent addresses, but the response was quite disappointing. No useful prints were obtained, and most recipients took no notice whatever of the request. I have since thought the question may have been confused with palmistry. It was not easy to get impressions from the paws of monkeys, apes, and lemuroids in Japan. Some few that were obtained at once betrayed a very strong similarity to those of man, and it seemed that a wider study would yield some hints, perchance, as to the path of man's ascent.

On the 15th February of the same year (1880), I wrote to the great pioneer in this field, Charles Darwin, sending specimens of prints and some outline of my first tentative results, and requesting him to aid me in obtaining access to imprints from lemurs, lemuroids, monkeys and anthropoid apes, as I had found them to show lineation patterns which I hoped might be serviceable to elucidate in some degree the lineage of man. I had failed to find any trace of references to these phenomena in any anatomical or biological work within reach. The few Oriental works I had seen were full of absurd phantasies and were allied to palmistry, but contained Buddhist and Taouist figures nowhere to be found in nature.

The great naturalist's reply, in his own handwriting, sent to me two years before his death, was as follows :—

" *Via* BRINDISI.
April 7th, 1880.

DOWN,
BECKENHAM, KENT,
RAILWAY STATION,
ORPINGTON, S.E.R.

" DEAR SIR,

" The subject to which you refer in your letter of February 15th seems to me a curious one, which may turn out interesting; but I am sorry to say that I am most unfortunately situated for offering you any assistance. I live in the country, and from weak health seldom see anyone. I will, however, forward your letter to Mr. F. Galton, who is the most likely man that I can think of to take up the subject to make further enquiries.

"Wishing you success,

"I remain, dear Sir,

"Yours faithfully,

"(*Signed*) CHARLES DARWIN."

This letter, with the envelope addressed by Mr. Darwin himself, and showing its postmarks, is in the library of the Royal Faculty of Physicians and Surgeons. Mr. F. Galton, afterwards Sir Francis Galton, a cousin of Charles Darwin, wrote in *Finger-Prints*, which was published by him in 1892, that his "attention was first drawn to the ridges in 1888 when preparing a lecture on Personal Identification for the Royal Institution, which had for its principal object an account of the anthropometric method of Bertillon, then newly introduced into the prison administration of France." [p. 2.]

In *Nature*, October 28th, 1880, appeared my article which was indexed shortly afterwards as the first contribution on the subject, in the *Index Medicus* of the United States, thus: "Faulds, H.—On the skin-furrows of the hand, *Nature*, London, xxii, 605."

Professor Otto Schlaginhaufen, while my *Guide* was going through the press in England, published in the August number of *Gegenbaur's Jahrbüch* for 1905 a copiously illustrated and well-informed article on the lineations in human beings, lemuroids, apes and anthropoids. The writer does me the honour of stating (p. 584) that with my contribution to *Nature* in 1880, there begins a new period in the investigation of the lineations of the skin, that, namely, in which they were brought into the service of criminal anthropology and medical jurisprudence. This publication, he says, is the forerunner of a copious literature which flowed over into the popular magazines and daily press, and promises to keep no bounds. He thinks that I pointed the right way to attain a knowledge of man's genetic descent by a study of the corresponding lineations of certain lower animals, such as lemuroids, and that I had suggested other directions in which medical jurisprudence might profitably engage in the study of this subject. A claim was shortly afterwards made in *Nature*, by Sir William Herschel, that he had, prior to my efforts, taken finger-prints for identification in India. I have entered into this personal matter elsewhere. Sir William has more than once publicly conceded priority of publication to me, and that is not at all disputable. We quite independently reached similar conclusions. Schlaginhaufen sums up the matter at least impartially, thus :—

> "Zeitlich erschien die Publikation FAULDS' früher; aber HERSCHEL wies durch die Veröffentlichung eines halboffiziellen Briefes nach dass er sich schon 1877 mit dem Gegendstand beschäftigt habe. Jedenfalls sind beide Beobachter unabhängig voneinander auf die gleiche Idee gekommen, und wenn auch die Materialien, die HERSCHEL lieferte, für die kriminelle Anthropologie speziell von grösserer Bedeutung waren, so hat FAULDS' doch in seiner ersten Mitteilung die Erforschung der Hautleisten von einem höheren Gesichtspunkt aus erfasst und ihr in einem umfassenderen Plan den Weg vorgezeichnet."

That is to say :—

> "Faulds's publication was earlier in time, but Herschel showed by the publication of a half-official

letter that he had been engaged with the method from 1877 onwards. In any case both observers had independently come to the same idea, and while the material which Herschel supplied was of greater service for criminal anthropology, Faulds had in his first communication grasped the investigation of the skin lineations from a higher standpoint, and had indicated the way to it through a more comprehensive plan."

My own plan laid stress on the serial imprint of five or ten fingers according to the size of the registers anticipated. Sir William Herschel used one, two, or three fingers only, and chiefly as sign-manuals. Sir William has since published a hand imprint used as a sign-manual and printed in 1858. On seeing the announcement I wrote to the publishers, who regretted they could not supply me with a copy as it was printed for private circulation only. Sir William Herschel has nowhere claimed to have had any methodic way of storing or indexing the records, and indeed, from his indications, they cannot have been at all numerous.

In 1887 and 1888, after my final return to England, I brought the method under the notice of the Home Authorities, who merely dealt with it in the usual red-tape methods. Finally, I asked to have one of their most intelligent officers appointed to meet me, so that I might enter fully into practical details. In reply there came to me a gentleman who sent in his official

J. B. TUNBRIDGE,
Inspector
C.I. DEPARTMENT, GREAT SCOTLAND YARD

card, which I have in my possession now. This was the able officer so well known by his dramatic capture of Mr. Jabez Balfour. I showed him how printing was done, the method of classification adopted by me, and offered to form a model bureau from the hands of the London police. A few years ago Mr. Tunbridge wrote me :—

> "I have a most distinct and pleasant recollection of our interview, and since the 'F. P.' system has been adopted as a means of identification of criminals with such marked success, have often wondered how it was that you have not been more actively connected with the carrying out of the system. When the Home Authorities recognized the value of the system, I was Commissioner of Police in New Zealand, and it was owing mainly to my recommendation that the system was introduced into the New Zealand prisons, although the Prison Authorities were somewhat opposed to it. . . Some of the Australian States also adopted the system, with the result that an interchange of prints took place, which soon manifested its value. The system is now in full working order in Australia, and is carried on by the police, of course, with the assistance of the Prison Authorities."

No report has been published of Mr. Tunbridge's impressions. At the close of our long interview he told me he was disposed to think the method would be rather delicate for practical application by the police, and that fresh legislation would be required before any beginning could be made.

In 1897, the finger-print system associated with Monsieur Bertillon's anthropometric system was adopted in India ; but soon the bodily measurements were abandoned, and the finger-print method alone was officially employed ; and in 1901 it was tentatively used in England and Wales, but did not come into much public use till a year or two afterwards. The ten-finger method in serial order, as I had from the first recommended for a large register, and prepared forms to receive imprints (as shown in *facsimile*), was adopted and is that now in official use. The methods of Sir William Herschel, followed by that of Sir F. Galton, were much more restricted, and could never have been worked practically in anything but a very small and limited register.

The finger-print system of identification is all but universally applied now throughout the civilized world for criminal cases, and bids fairly well to be soon adopted for other methods of identification than that of professional criminals or recidivists. After great earthquakes, floods, or battles, multitudes of people have to be hastily buried who have never been fully identified. In such cases the existence of a civil or military Finger-print Register would be a very great means of security, and this it is my great wish to see recognized and established.

I wish to make it clear that in 1880 no printed proposal existed to use finger-prints for identification. Sir F. Galton has referred to a United States expedition in which the method was used, but the date was 1882, and the example printed could not identify. He also refers to Mr. Tabor, of San Francisco, who had proposed the registration of Chinamen by this method, as their identity was difficult to establish. I believe this also was in 1882. In a criticism of Dr. Schlaginhaufen's Bibliography (" F.G. " is the signature) in *Nature*, the omission of Mr. Tabor's name is regretted, but why? Did he write on the subject anything which has been preserved? Why, before this period, Dr. Billings, of the United States Army, said at the International Medical Congress : " Just as each individual is in some respects peculiar and unique, so that even the minute ridges and furrows at the end of his fore-fingers differ from that of all other forefingers, and is sufficient to identify," etc. So that in America the matter was widely known, and Dr. Billings' own work on the " Index " attributed its initiation to me.

Again, in 1883, " Mark Twain " published his charming *Life on the Mississippi*, a very valuable human document. It contains a well-thought-out story of an identification by means of a thumb-print on a system supposed by him to have been invented by a French prison doctor. His *Pudd'nhead Wilson*, in which a still better study of the subject occurs, did not come out till 1894, the year in which the sitting of Mr. Asquith's Committee on Identification of Habitual Criminals had set journalists agoing again on the theme of " thumb-prints." Prior to that year a great deal had been written on the subject, the facts being chiefly taken from the correspondence in *Nature*, to which reference has been made.

CHAPTER II

SWEAT-PORES, RIDGES AND FURROWS

THE front or palmar surface of human hands, and the corresponding solar or plantar surface of the feet, are marked with alternate ridges and furrows, lying for the most in nearly parallel rows, but often again at certain points on palm or sole, curving, splitting, twisting, or joining to form patterns of much intricacy. The ridges, called technically *rugæ* (sing. *ruga*), are punctuated at very frequent intervals with small openings, which are the mouths or pores of the sweat ducts connected with certain glands which lie deep in the lower strata of the skin. The furrows or *sulci* (sing. *sulcus*) are almost devoid of any such apertures. There are probably some two or three millions of those tiny sweat pores in a human body, which afford an evaporating surface, according to the anatomist Krause, of about eight square inches. The sweat is a watery, slightly saline fluid, with slight

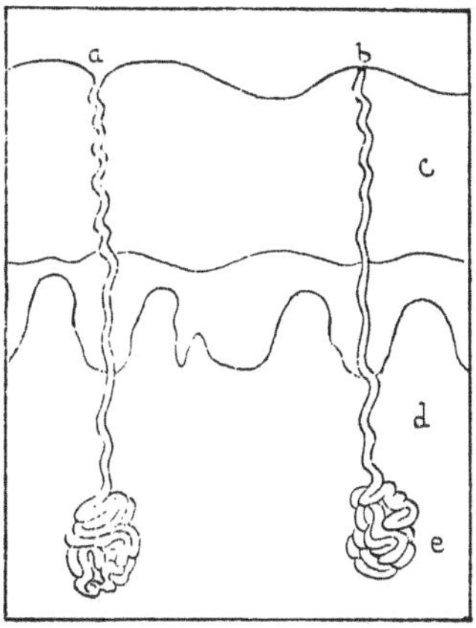

SECTION OF SKIN, SHOWING SWEAT-GLANDS, DUCTS AND PORES

a. pore open.
b. pore closed.
d. sweat duct.
e. sweat gland.

—very slight—traces of grease, some small cell-like particles, and some carbonic acid and other gaseous matters, which exhale from the skin. The more oily secretion of the skin comes from a different set of openings with their associated glands, the sebaceous glands, which are associated with the hairy surfaces of the body. In Ludwig Hopf's work, *The Human Species*, the subject is discussed fully. When the palmar surface leaves a distinctly greasy impression, this greasiness must have been acquired from outside or from transmitted exudation from the back or dorsal surfaces, or other parts of the body.

Those skin ridges, apart from any relation they may have either to the sweat-pores or to the special nerves of touch and temperature which lie near them, serve a useful purpose in helping the horny hands of toil to grasp its tools firmly. They occur in a few other parts of animals somewhat near to us in the scale of being. A striking example is that on the palmar surface of the prehensile or grasping tail of the Spider Monkey (*Ateles ater*), which it uses in climbing almost like a hand.

When the ridges in human fingers are well softened with water, and are then rubbed along the surface of a tumbler or wine-glass, musical sounds may be elicited, which are caused by the alternate resistance and yielding of the softened ridges. This was the principle of the " musical glasses " of Goldsmith's time. The navvy often begins his labours by moistening his loof. After his efforts make him perspire, he has no further need in this way for his salivary resources. Hence Nature, too, has placed the openings of the sweat-pores on the crests of his ridges, and not, as Herbert Spencer on one occasion is said to have supposed she had done, in the troughs of the furrows, where they are very seldom to be found, and would not be nearly so useful. Curiously enough, our modern makers of indiarubber tyres work a trade-mark pattern or title in ridges on their wares, so as to secure a good grip on the road—and on the market. In a similar way the carriers of Manchuria adorn their clumsy wheels with studs to prevent their skidding.

There are, as has been mentioned, two kinds of minute glands in the skin: one, to secrete that complex excretion, the sweat; the other, to provide a certain greasiness to hair. The latter are found chiefly in other parts than the palms, and serve to secure that slight oiliness of the surface of our bodies which is very well seen in taking one's bath. However thoroughly that thin film of surface greasiness is removed with the use of soap and vigorous scrubbing, in a moment or two water is seen to act on the cutaneous surface as it would on a slightly greasy platter or a duck's back. The importance of this point will become apparent when we come to deal with some practical applications of dactylography in searching for invisible greasy finger-marks, which may be made visible.

Looking carefully at the visible texture of the fingers and palms, we see, then, that the cutaneous ridges lie, for the most part, closely and evenly, like furrows in a well-ploughed field. But just as in some fields the ploughman has perforce had to swerve and veer round some fast embedded boulder or old tree stump, varying his intended pattern, so, too, in our fingers curious divergent lineations are found to occur, and we cannot very well tell the reason why. Coloured patches may be designed like so many pretty wall-paper designs, to enclose these patterns in books on finger-prints, but I, for one, cannot see that they throw any light on their genuine nature and origin. We find, under purely mechanical conditions, similar patterns produced in the ripples of a subaerial sand-drift and on a tidal shore. While writing this chapter, I saw to-day similar deltas, junctions, forks, and the like, on a lake whose frozen surface was

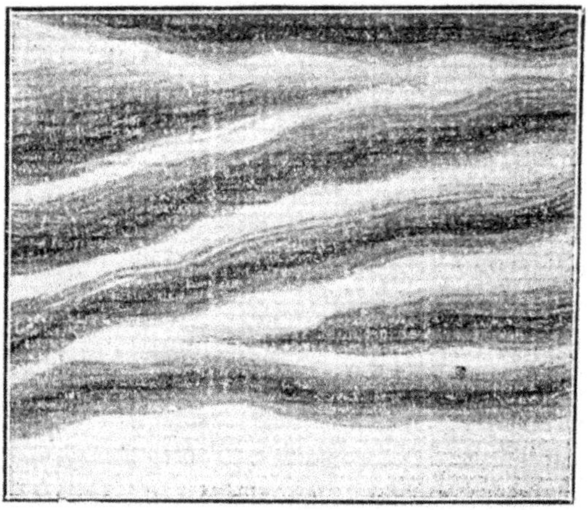

RIPPLE MARKS IN SAND (*After*, *Lyell*).

thinly sprinkled with fine dry snow. The lines were mostly parallel, but where certain gusts or eddies had occurred they had been broken up into patterns not unlike those of finger-tips.

In human skin, and in the anthropoid apes, those scroll-like patterns present almost infinite varieties of detail, and they often resemble a condensed railway plan, showing junctions, blind sidings, loops, triangles, and curves. There is one important distinction to be observed. The lineations of skin ridges are not always quite uniform in breadth, but broaden out sometimes or dwindle away. Again, they are dotted with sweat-pores and do not always, when printed from, show those pores in the same degree of patency or openness. Hence a little variation is inevitable when the same finger is several times impressed under varying conditions. It is not to be forgotten that, to a limited extent, this is true of a rigid box-wood engraving or steel plate, or lithographic stone, which give somewhat divergent results with varying degrees of pressure in printing, moisture of atmosphere or paper, and other conditions.

In this country the feet do not afford a favourable field of study to the dactylographer. So far as identification is concerned, little use could be made of them practically. In the East, however, it is different, and many years' residence there gave me opportunities to observe that the toes, unrestrained by the use of stiff leather boots, are mobile and powerful, grasping as fingers do. The carpenter in Japan, for example, uses his toes to grip and steady the board he is sawing or hewing, while many of my readers must be familiar with the extraordinary agility of Japanese acrobats in the use of their feet and toes. In those cases the ridges are often varied in grouping, and well defined in development. A European baby generally begins life with similar simian-like powers. But so far as my own observations go, the patterns in the hands usually show a somewhat higher degree of evolution, a more complex and intricate network of lines, than those exhibited by the feet of the same person. Hence, apart from the greater convenience of inspecting them, the finger-prints have greater value for the purpose of identification. Cases, however, of crime, might readily occur even in this country, where the imprints of naked feet might yield important and irrefutable evidence of one's presence at a scene of evil-doing.

But there are other important points of scientific interest besides their evidential value for identification. An important problem in evolutionary development, on which a considerable amount of literature begins to accumulate, is the serial relation of the limbs. Professor Bowditch, the distinguished biologist, of Harvard University, U.S., wrote me, of date November 18th, 1880, thus:—

> "DEAR SIR,—I have just read in *Nature* of October 28th, your article on the skin-furrows of the hand. The subject interested me because it so happened that fourteen years ago, at the suggestion of the late Professor Jeffries Wyman, I made some prints of the finger and toe tips with the hope of throwing some light on the question of the antero-posterior symmetry of the body. Since reading your article I have made some new impressions from the same individual, and it is interesting to notice the unchanged character of the cutaneous furrows."

Some additional particulars are added in the letter, and a fine finger imprint was enclosed.

It is well to remember that the comparison of the ridges to those of a ploughed field does not always, and in every way, hold good. As I have elsewhere said: *

> "The lines are not of uniform width. Ofttimes they may be likened rather to the mountains and valleys in a good survey. The ridges sometimes split or send little spurs down into the neighbouring valleys; at other times a ridge seems to cleave, giving rise to a form

* *Guide to Finger-Print Identification* (p. 11).

like a tarn or lake in a limestone range: here and there solitary islands rise in the valleys, and sometimes quite an archipelago takes the place of some of the commoner patterns. Indeed, the ordinary nomenclature of an ordinary physical geography map may be found quite helpful in laying a case clearly before a magistrate or a jury. And just as we find in the case of mountains and valleys in a map, every variety of shape may occur in a finger-pattern."

Here it may be as well to state, as we shall see more precisely further on, that an English jury is well enabled to judge of the conformity of two patterns, one of which is suspect only, and the other officially printed from the fingers of some one in custody —by great photographic enlargement of the exhibits in the case, used as evidence.

The ridges, as may be seen by an enlarged photograph (as on frontispiece), do not always continue to be of quite uniform width throughout. Sometimes they taper away sharply like a railway point, or trickle off in diminishing dots; or again, especially where something like triangles occur, called deltas (after the Greek letter, Δ *delta*), they flatten out in breadth considerably. In old age they are found usually to have partaken of the general drying up and shrivelling of the tissues.

In the cold or shivering stage of ague and fevers, and in the affection called Reynaud's disease, in which the fingers may tend to become pale and bloodless, some slight shrinking of the ridges also takes place, a point which might be of importance in the measurement of enlarged exhibits in the trial, for example, of an old Indian soldier or traveller who had been subject to fits of ague.

I have heard Sir A. Moseley Channel, who has

informed himself well about finger-print matters, in a charge to a jury in a murder case, refer to the doubtful and unsatisfactory nature of evidence from a print done by a sweaty finger.

The fact that sweaty finger-marks have been adduced in evidence of crime makes it important for lawyers, police officials, judges and jurymen, to understand what is meant by such natural records. A mark from pure sweat would necessarily be excessively transient, as it consists chiefly of water and salines, and should properly contain no greasy matter whatever. Dr. Reginald Alcock, of the North Stafford Infirmary, in a recent paper read at Stoke-on-Trent, and since re-published in *The British Medical Journal*, described his researches into the relation of the sweat-pores to practical surgery, and to the recognized difficulty in sterilising the skin for subsequent operation. Dr. Alcock shows that there may often be found remaining, after the best efforts to cleanse the surface, a stubborn residue of live and obnoxious matter in those tiny invisible ducts, matter which had insidiously gained entrance from without. Now such decaying or dead particles of foreign protoplasm would, I think, readily enough account for the very faint traces of oily matter sometimes observed, which oiliness makes sweat from a skin, fair and clean in the ordinary sense, leave slight but somewhat persistent traces on such substances as glass and the like.

In a case reported some time ago, in *The Birmingham Post*, Detective-Sergeant Charles Munro, on cross-examination as to a sweaty smudge left on glass, said: "The impressions on the window-pane were sweat-marks. They had conducted experiments in Scotland

Yard, and ascertained that sweat-marks lasted on glass for a week if not exposed to the wind." Here, I suppose, the distinction between a sweat-mark proper and a somewhat greasy sweat-mark was not discerned. Even a deliberately designed greasy mark is volatile to a certain extent just as the oil of new paint dries in a day or two according to the weather.

In the *Guide* (p. 65) I have alluded to the fact of coloured sweat or *Chromidrosis*, thus :—

> "A blackish ooze takes place in some hysterical cases. More striking is the class of cases in which the colouring matter is derived, like the bright colours in the plumage of parrots, from copper, and in some cases from iron. Workers in copper have been found subject to it. The sweat is generally of a bluish colour in those cases. Red sweat has been observed in lockjaw. A kind of saffron colour I have found to be not very uncommon in some classes of malarious cases. One lady I attended had an extraordinary temperature during some of the attacks, the thermometer recording 110° Fahrenheit. With a temperature of about 104° Fahr. she did not seem to be really unwell. I took good impressions at one of those times, with the yellow-coloured sweat. Ordinarily, however, sweat does not help, but hinder, impressions from being made. A case of blue sweat came under my treatment quite recently. There was no history of copper poisoning."

Since writing the above, I have met with other cases of coloured sweat. My teacher, the late Sir Thomas McCall Anderson, in his work, *Contributions to Clinical Medicine*, mentions some very interesting facts in this connection in the chapter on "Hemidrosis."

Herbert Spencer, in the May number of the *Nineteenth Century* (1886), discussing the Factors of Organic Evolution, explains the origin of the ridges in a passage which I must quote in full :—

" Continuous pressure on any portion of the surface causes absorption, while intermittent pressure causes growth : the one impeding circulation and the passage of plasma from the capillaries into the tissues, and the other aiding both. There are yet further mechanically produced effects. That the general character of the ribbed skin on the under-surfaces of the feet and inside of the hands, is directly due to friction and intermitten pressure, we have the proofs : first, that the tracks most exposed to rough usage are the most ribbed ; second, that the insides of hands subject to unusual amounts of rough usage, as those of sailors, are strongly ribbed all over ; and third, that in hands which are very little used, the parts commonly ribbed become quite smooth."

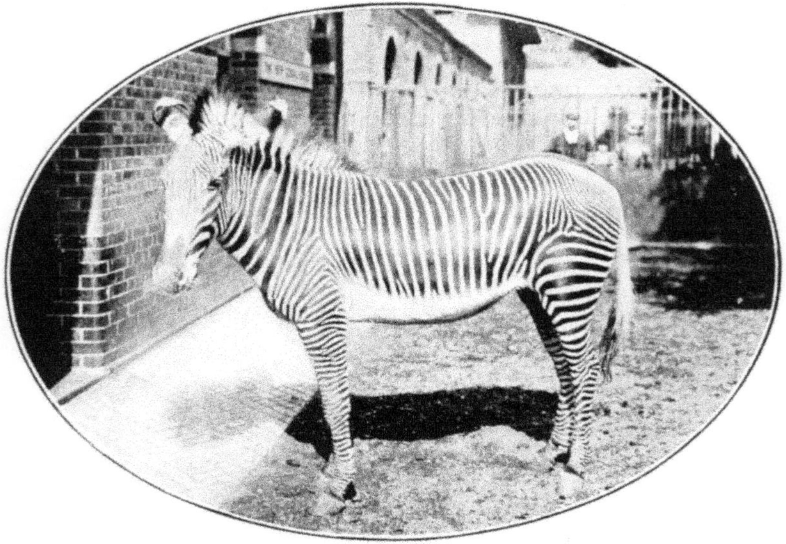

GREVY'S ZEBRA.—Showing Lineations like Finger-Print Patterns.

Dactylography, opposite p. 39]

[Photo. Pictorial Agency

CHAPTER III

FINGER-PRINT PATTERNS

BEFORE reading this chapter, let the reader carefully examine the clear lineations shown so well in the photographic picture of the Zebra's stripes, opposite. They will be found to resemble very closely the lineations on the skin of human fingers, as printed when enlarged by photography, forming very similar patterns. Similar linings occur in the hide of the tiger.

Where two lines, beginning as parallels, curve to divide, a fresh line begins to appear between. Sometimes a single line forks into two or three. Again, triangular arrangements of lineations are seen on the zebra, and one can trace some of these back into lines running as a parallel series. Surely the causes which produce the ridges on a human or anthropoid finger cannot be quite the same biologically as lead to the formation of similar patterns in the skin of the zebra. There are mechanical or physical conditions, however, which condition the formation of ridges in a sandy shore, of powdery snow blown by the wind and tossed on a smooth frozen lake, as has already been noticed, and these conditions are being carefully elucidated by scientific observers. But why living tissues should produce patterns like those, just in those positions, and then reproduce them in living descendants with slight but important variations, is a totally different question, the answer to which must be reached in a different way.

While the ridges and furrows lie in parallels or curve in the same direction over some considerable surface of the sole and palm, they also gather up into more or less intricate, scroll-like patterns at various points besides those of the last joints of the fingers, which have chiefly engrossed popular attention hitherto. In man, the lemurs, lemuroids, and apes, these pattern points are numerous. In my own hands, there are on the left hand, besides the five finger-tip patterns, other five like them, and the right hand contains six. There are thus twenty-one *complex* patterns which might be used for identification.

On the other hand, when one reads of a mathematical attempt to compute the probabilities of two finger-prints being alike, it is not a question simply of comparing an unknown finger smudge with collections containing ten finger-prints each, for the unknown smudge may have been made, not from one of a possible set of ten finger-tip prints, but from one of those other local patterns not on the finger-tips at all. There is a saying often attributed to Huxley, who certainly used it wisely, that the value of grist from the mathematical mill depends on the quality of the corn put into the hopper. But official amateur mathematicians have made many much worse mistakes than the above in regard to probabilities in the realm of finger-print evidence.

In a few cases, especially in the feet patterns, often a very plain character, parallel or slightly wavy lines of no precise design, so to speak, may be found. A short time ago, when applying mustard to the feet of a lady in some kind of fit, I observed this almost featureless pattern in her toes. If such cases were as common in the hands as they are rare, the finger-print method would hardly be of any avail for identification. A teleologist of the old school of Paley might argue with some plausibility that the possible usefulness of those intricate patterns was the true meaning of their existence, otherwise not yet explainable. That the old Paleyan conception of nature having an end or purpose in view, the teleological explanation of things as useful to the being possessing them, had its own usefulness in giving a broader view of natural history facts in their inter-relations, is borne out even by so great an authority as Charles Darwin himself. Are the markings in a bird's eggs recognized by the sitting bird in those cases where the markings are peculiar—and some are like written characters—or are they purely accidental and useless? A correspondent in *The Country-Side* wrote a short time ago, describing a test case he observed of a thrush in his possession. This bird built a nest and laid therein five eggs, "varying in size from a good-sized pea to the normal size. The smaller ones I took away and substituted one from a wild bird's nest; this the following day I found laid at the bottom of the aviary smashed. I again repeated the addition with the same result. I had carefully marked the eggs, so that there could be no mistake." The writer signed himself "W. A., Wimbledon."

Dr. Wallace's view, as I understand it, is that variations in wild animals were due chiefly to immunity from enemies, allowing free play to the natural tendency to variation, kept only in check by its dangers, such as leading to betrayal by conspicuous colouring, and so on.

Professor Poulton in *The Colours of Animals*, 2nd ed. p. 212, says :—

> " It is very probable that the great variation in the colours and markings of birds' eggs, which are laid close together in immense numbers, may possess this significance, enabling each bird to know its own eggs. I owe this suggestive interpretation to my friend, Mr. Francis Gotch : it is greatly to be hoped that experimental confirmation may be forthcoming. The suggestion could be easily tested by altering the position of the eggs and modifying their appearance by painting. Mr. Gotch's hypothesis was formed after seeing a large number of eggs of the guillemot in their natural surroundings."

Australian ewes know the bleat of their own lambs, however immense the flock, and all through nature we find this useful note of recognition. One of the most philosophic interpreters of living phenomena, viewing things from a very recent standpoint—Professor J. Arthur Thomson, in his fascinating *Biology of the Seasons* (p. 174), writing of the colour and texture of birds' eggs, says :—

> " In some cases, it is said, the shell registers hybridism—a very remarkable fact. It is another illustration of the great, though still vague, truth that the living creature is a unity through and through, specific even in the structure of the egg-shell within which it is developed. For although the shell is secreted by the walls of the oviduct, it seems to be in some measure controlled by the life of the giant-cell—the ovum—within."

Such pattern-forming qualities are found in many fields of nature, very beautifully, for example, as we have seen, in the skin of the zebra ; on the back of a mackerel ; in the grain of various kinds of wood ; in the veining of leaves and petals ; and in the covering or substance of seeds such as the nutmeg and scarlet runner bean. Sir Charles Lyell, in his *Elements of Geology*, figures the ribbing of sand on the sea-shore in a wood-cut which might be an enlarged diagram of human skin. (See fig. on page 32). In his *Principles of Geology* (5th ed., vol. i., p. 323) there is, again, a figure described as a section of " spheroidal concretionary Travertine," which contains many linings strikingly like those with which we have to deal in this little work.

It follows from these analogies that a method of analysing and classifying such patterns might have very wide utilities beyond its relation to finger-prints. It is easy, for example, to recognize the same zebra in quite different pictures. Another point of practical importance is this, that a smudgy or blotchy impression, supposed to be that of a criminal present at some seat of crime, might be the impressed copy merely of some object or texture other than human skin, but containing lineations of similar arrangement. An outworn transversely cut branch of a tree might readily produce a print like that of a human finger. An expert would probably notice that in the lineations there were no real junctions, each woody ring remaining apart from the others; but, again, there are some human fingers of such patterns. I think the bloody smear officially reproduced as impressed on a post-card in facsimile,

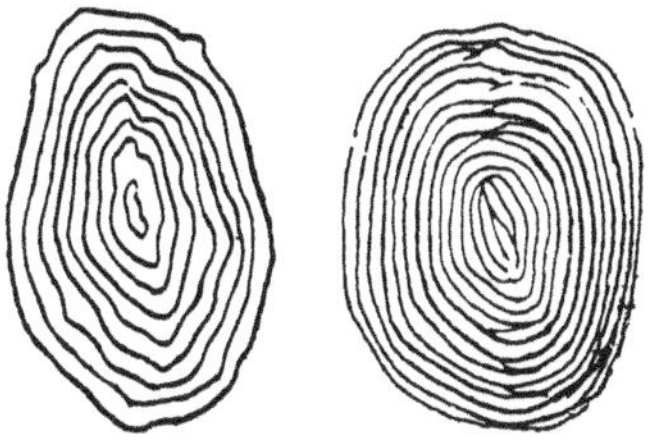

a b

a. section of pine-wood stem. *b.* a human thumb-print.

and purporting to have come from "Jack the Ripper," at the time of the Whitechapel horrors in the eighties, may have been produced by the sleeve of a twilled coat smeared with blood. It contained no characters specially characteristic of skin lineations, which it was presumed to be an example of, as impressed.

Apart from all that, lemurs, lemuroids, apes, anthropoids, and monkeys, all show on hands and feet, skin lineations in patterns similar to those of man. In the anthropoid apes it would not be easy to discriminate them from those of human beings. Some of these were figured in my *Guide*, and Dr. Otto Schlaginhaufen has supplied numerous good prints.

If Edgar A. Poe, in his famous mystery of evil deeds done by a gigantic ape, had been acquainted with finger-print methods, he might have pictured the police as still more mystified by the imprints of seemingly human hands.

There are two methods of observing systematically the lineation patterns.

1.—*The Direct Mode.*—This might be done simply by many people by looking at the lineations with the unaided vision. Till quite recently the author found no difficulty in doing this, with myopic eyes that could see something of the texture of a house-fly's eyes in a good light. My earliest observations of the finger-patterns were made in this way, while the patterns were reproduced in pencilled outlines. The condition of the actual ridges and furrows themselves, with their open and acting or closed and dormant sweat-pores, ought to be familiar to the student of dactylography, who is apt to narrow his vision by the contemplation only of dead impressions made in ink or otherwise. A lens such as botanists use for field work is very useful, and a high power is neither necessary nor very helpful. Drawings of the patterns ought to be made from time to time with coloured or "lead" pencils, and those drawings should be accurately adjusted by the use of rubber and compasses.

2.—*The Indirect Method.*—This is done by the medium of casts and printed impressions. Casts may be made of clay, putty, sealing-wax, beeswax, gutta-percha, hard paraffin, varnish, half-dry paint, and the like. Printed impressions or dactylographs may be obtained from greasy or sweaty fingers, blood, printer's ink, or various substitutes for it.

Within this method, again, two very distinct and complementary kinds of results may be obtained, which I have elsewhere described as Positive and Negative. The first or Positive is that, for example, which is used officially for the record of convicted prisoners by printing with ordinary printer's ink, just as a veined leaf or fern, or a box-wood engraving is printed from. Here the ridges or raised lines appear black on a white ground, while the intervening furrows appear white, as do also the minute pores dotted along the crest of each ridge. (See frontispiece.)

In the other method, as when the fingers are impressed on a carefully smoked surface of glass, the projecting ridges lift up the carbon of the soot, leaving a white pattern behind, with the sweat-pores forming black punctuations, while the receding furrows leave the black surface untouched. When such impressions have to be used again, as for evidence, they should be carefully varnished, as they are exceedingly liable to be destroyed by the slightest contact.

In a case under judicial investigation where an official imprint had to be compared with one done by accident negatively on smoked glass or the like, the black lineations would not closely correspond—would, in fact, considerably diverge in pattern. This might tend to confuse judge and jury if the distinction of negative and positive dactylograph were not made clear by the expert witness. Then the apparent divergences could easily be demonstrated to be very significant coincidences.

Five years of my early life were spent in learning a trade in Glasgow—that of the soon-to-be-obsolete Paisley shawl manufacture. It seemed to me to have been an utter waste of time, but part of my duty was to deal with the arrangement, classifying, and numbering immense varieties of patterns, printed with every conceivable variation of combined colours. It was impossible to carry these on memory, and one had to resort to mnemonic means of classification.

Now, the immense significance of the variety in human finger-patterns dawned upon me very early, when I had once begun to interest myself in them.

There are many patterns, which, when analysed into their composing elements, present analogies to artistic designs, a view which is no mere personal fad, but has been affirmed with enthusiasm by many artists in designs to whom I have pointed out those figures. Here are a few, by way of illustrating this point (space will not permit of more). Those figures are from real human finger-prints rendered diagrammatically. This is the first step, then, to catch with the eye the pattern or

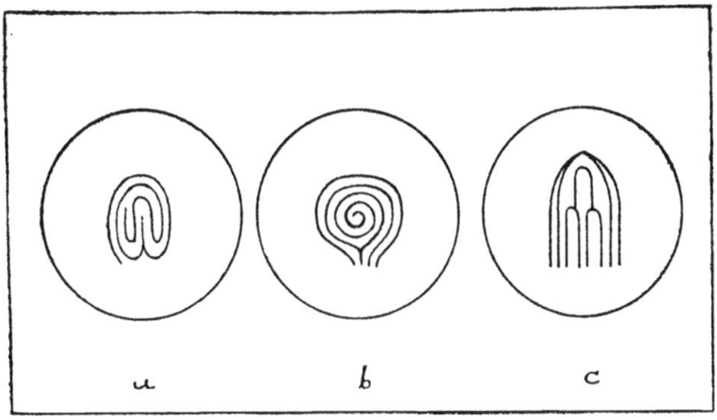

DESIGN-LIKE PATTERNS IN FINGER-PRINTS No. 1.
(Diagrammatic)

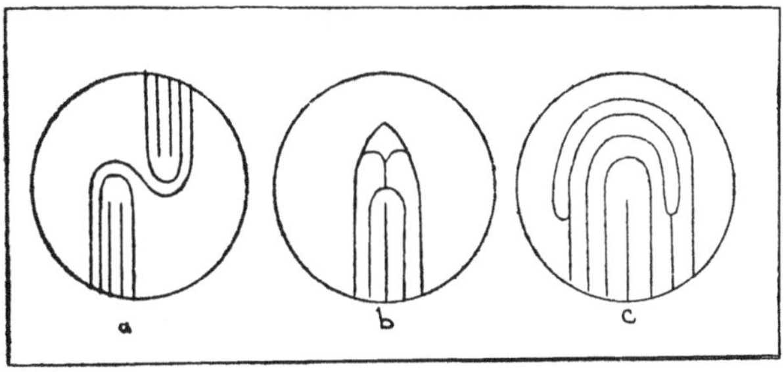

DESIGN-LIKE PATTERNS No. 2.

design; give it a class name, and you have at once established some practical basis of classification in finger-prints. Then it is possible to frame some kind of catalogue for reference arranged like a dictionary with its sub-alphabetic order, in an almost infinite series. The initial difficulty is generally that which arises from want of skill in printing, which technical points will be considered subsequently. A soft and flexible substance like the ridges in human fingers does not always yield an exactly similar impression in two successive moments, under varying conditions of temperature, fatigue, and the like. Nor does the analogy of mathematical diagrams always fitly apply in such a case. Even in steel engravings and fine etchings, as the connoisseur well knows, the degree of intensity of the pressure and other conditions will modify to some slight extent the resulting imprint, but what I wish to emphasize is, that if the original pattern had any value at all resulting from its complexity as a pattern, the variation in printing as now done officially by experienced police officials will not impair much its value as evidence of personal identity in a court of law. Even the amateur will soon, after a little practice with good materials, attain a very fair amount of clearness and uniformity in his imprints.

CHAPTER IV

SOME BIOLOGICAL QUESTIONS IN DACTYLOGRAPHY.

In this chapter I propose to bring together a few important points of a biological character, which are so vital that even in so curtailed a discussion they cannot be ignored. We shall also glance—it must literally be the merest glance—at the problem of man's genetic descent, in so far as it begins now to be illumined, however faintly, by a comparative study of finger-prints. Comparatively little of a final character has as yet been achieved, but there are now not a few active and intelligent observers in many lands, and the scientific results often attained under the greatest difficulties are so far greatly encouraging. Fortunately the day has long passed away when it can be considered irreverent to enquire modestly as to who were one's ancestors. In a very true biological sense every human individual is known to have run through a scale of existence, beginning from the lowest mono-cellular organism, through something like a tadpole or salamander, into a vertebrate and mammal type, not easily to be discriminated from the undeveloped young of rat, or pig, or monkey. Now, if he is not in any way individually degraded by this actually demonstrable course of development, why should he be thought racially degraded by an honest scientific effort to trace the origin of his species from lowly animal ancestry? The process may be slower, but is no less determined by divinely established law. Our grandfathers believed that the Creator breathed into the organized and shapely form of Adam (=" a man ") a portion of the divine spirit, by which he became a living soul, and forthwith took his dignified place in nature. To me the old story, when retold in more modern and exact phrase, leads us to an entirely hopeful and inspiring conception of the origin and evolutionary destiny of our race.

When we approach the threshold of man's first appearance on the globe, we have reached a geologic epoch when our sober earth seems to have sown most of its wild oats. Its " crust " is pretty stable, and at least in its broad distribution of sea and land, it does not seem to differ very greatly from what its appearance presents on a modern physiographical map. Minor differences there must have been, as even our modern English coast-line shows, and there may have been other conditions than now exist to account for many of man's early migrations, but those differences are still matters of discussion. There were, possibly, enough certain bridge-like links between lands now apart and separated by wide stretches of sea, but, as a rule, such conclusions have been deductively reached, and are not definitely established on scientific evidence.

After rising above one-celled to more complicated organisms, we reach a class of creatures in which a radiate or wheel-like form obtains, that is, radial symmetry, as in jelly-fish, star-fish, urchins, and sea-anemones.

Fishes occupy, perhaps, about the lowest level among the back-boned or vertebrate animals, and we may readily notice that some of their fins occur in symmetrically arranged pairs, while others, again, occur singly. Now with this arrangement of such appendages in pairs symmetrically arranged there begins the appearance of something definitely like what we mean by limbs. Some present-day fishes use some of their fins as legs to clamber and crawl on rocks or ashore. I remember seeing, in a Japanese tea-house by the solitary sea-shore, not far from where the great arsenal of Yokoska now hums busily, a very beautiful gurnard, blue as to its outspread wings like the sapphire gurnard. Those fins were painted like the wings of a butterfly, and it crawled about in the limited sea-water, on rocks, under cliffs, and among sea-weed, with butterfly-like legs or processes from the roots of those wing-like fins. With such a special adaptation of their fins, fishes began to conquer the land. Seals and whales, as is well known, are mammals which have been driven back again to the sea.

Thesing, in his suggestive *Lectures on Biology* (English translation, p. 13), says :—

> " All extremities of the higher vertebrates, however widely they may differ in construction, may be traced back biogenetically to the so-called Ichthyopterygium, as we see it in the lower shark-like fishes. Unequal growth of the single skeleton parts and a considerable reduction in their numbers transformed the Ichthyopterygium into the five-fingered extremity characteristic of all vertebrates from the amphibians upwards."

Of course the great end of an animal is at first to fill its own belly, and in order to do this, if fixed as some molluscs are, it must contrive to bring nutriment within its reach, and if mobile limbs come to be developed to achieve locomotion, by fin in water, limb on land, and wing in air. After the vertebrate and mammal stage was achieved, the five-fingered limb takes various forms, as the paddle of the whale or wing of the bat. There are three great periods in geological development of animals —the Primary, which is, roughly speaking, the typical period of fishes; the Secondary, when reptiles prevail; and the Tertiary, the great age of mammals. Many geologists recognize a fourth period, the Post-Tertiary,

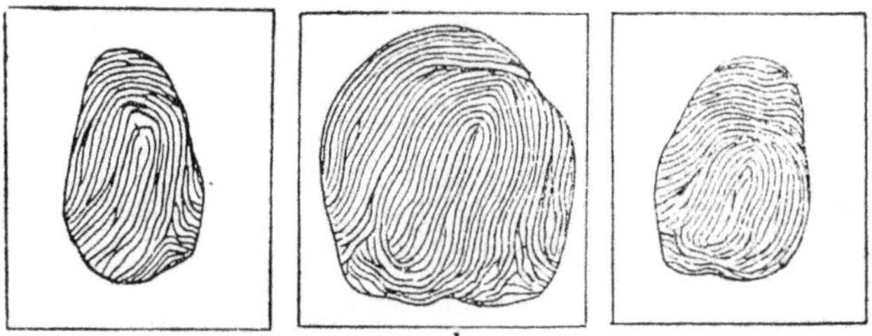

a *b* *c*

ANTHROPOID LINEATIONS.
a, from hand of orang, left index;
b, from foot of chimpanzee, left index;
c, from foot of orang, left index.

Quaternary, or Diluvian, when existing species have been established. It is not till this latest period has arrived that we can detect unmistakable evidences of man. There are, however, many reasons which lead to the conclusion that his racial roots go still further back in time. Did he arise as a "mutation," one of those rare sudden changes observed to take place even at the present time, by which a species suddenly departs from its ancestral type and is transformed? Let us briefly look at the main facts of mammalian ascent. The great herbivorous reptiles—some do not seem to have been strictly herbivorous—do not seem to lead us far on our path. Widely spread throughout the world, the Theriomorphs or beast-shaped reptiles seem to approach the mammal type, but they were too helpless and unwieldy, and had little brain-power wherewith to direct their energies. The earliest genuine mammals were small, not only relatively to those great creatures, but really little, rat-like rodents. Then we find arboreal creatures, driven to the trees for refuge and for food, squirrel-like animals, agile to escape from their monstrous but clumsy and stupid foes on the ground, and using their paws nimbly as hands to grasp and tear, or to break nuts and other food.

Lemur-like animals (lemuroids) then come on the stage, and among them—among the earliest of them—we begin to detect traces, on feet and hands, of those patterned ridges, the beginnings of which we have been seeking. Hand and brain and voice are the trinity of social construction. The spider and the mantis (or praying insect) have nimble, hand-like organs—very striking and conspicuous in the mantis; the chameleon among reptiles, the parrot among birds, the squirrel among lower mammals, all have somewhat hand-like organs used in hand-like ways; but when we reach the higher mammals, the sense of touch is finely intertwined with the power of varied and discriminative grasping, pressing, or rubbing. The elephant, which appears at first in the strata as about the size of a dog, grows in size and brain power as the ages roll along. But his path seems now to be closing. With his sagacious brain, and prehensile, sensitive trunk, he can do wonders, but, like the horse, he is likely to be passed by; the great tool-maker finding it easy now to make bearers swifter or more powerful than they are.

It is in man and the anthropoid apes that we first find the correspondence between hand and brain that promises mastery. The ugly, painted mandrill, even, has beautiful lady-like hands and takes care of them like a lady. All the higher apes show complicated finger-patterns like those of man.

The rugæ in apes and men seem clearly to have served a most useful purpose in aiding the firm grasp of hands or feet, a very vital point in creatures living an arboreal life, as they and their racial predecessors are now presumed to have done. In that case, however, would not one pattern, a simple one, have done as well as any other? Here, then, the great balancing principles of variation and heredity come into operation. The variety of patterns is immense, and for aught we know new ones may be being evolved at the present time. Here again, heredity comes in, for there is certainly some tendency to repeat in a quite general way the pattern of sire in the hands and feet of son. I have as yet found no quite close correspondence of detail in any case brought under my own notice. The question of identifying a person on one or two lineations involves so many practical problems of obscurity in printing and the like, that it is more appropriate for discussion in another chapter.

In a work published last year on *Science and the Criminal*, by Mr. C. Ainsworth Mitchell, after quoting a reference I made on one occasion to the influence of heredity in *sometimes* dominating finger-patterns, the author goes on to say: "While there is questionably a general tendency for a particular type of finger-prints to be inherited just as any other bodily peculiarities are liable to be passed on from the parents to the children, there is by no means that definite relationship that Dr. Faulds hoped to establish." The full passage in my paper in *Nature* referred to, was this :—

> "The dominancy of heredity through these infinite varieties is sometimes very striking. I have found unique patterns in a parent repeated with marvellous accuracy in his child. Negative results, however, might prove nothing in regard to parentage, a caution which it is important to make."

The truth is, I have very frequently emphasized the fact that in such similar patterns in sire and son there is no real danger of false identification where several fingers are compared in their proper serial order. It is not even likely that two such fingers would agree exactly in lineations, number, curvature, etc., if carefully measured in the way set forth in this work.

A more remarkable criticism is to be found in p. 63, thus: "The existence of racial peculiarities in finger-prints, which Dr. Faulds believed that he had discovered in the case of the Japanese, has not been borne out by the experience of others." The author then mentions some observations on this point by Galton, who thought that "the width of the ridges appeared to be more uniform and their direction more parallel in the finger-prints of negroes than in those of other races." The word "negroes" here is delightfully vague in an ethnological discussion. I have written nothing to justify the above remark. My belief has long been that there is *no* racial difference of yellow, white, red, or black, to use the good old Egyptian classification, but that the human family is one, and that view (right or wrong) was enunciated often by me in Japan, both by speech and pen. Mr. Mitchell's strange misconception must surely be based on my words in the article by me quoted above, where, after enumerating some elements in patterns from different races, I go on distinctly to say: "These instances are not intended to stand for typical patterns of the two peoples, but simply as illustrations of the kind of facts to be observed."

I had pleasure in giving my subscription and support to the recent First Universal Races Congress, which has done much, I believe, to consolidate scientific opinion as to the essential unity of our kind, a belief not so old or universal as many think, dating, indeed, not much more than a century back, if so far, as a scientific opinion, not biassed by the slave interest.

Of much more importance now is the relation to human beings to the great anthropoid stocks.

It is usual to separate the lemurs, which have strong affinities to monkeys and to men, from the anthropoids, or man-like apes, forming two great orders of

Lemuroidea, and
Anthropoidea.

In 1909, however, a paper was published by the Zoological Society of London, in which this separation is considered to be no longer justifiable, so that the lemurs and big man-like apes (orang, chimpanzee, and gorilla) would no longer be held as separate orders or sub-orders. There were some who hoped to show that the races of men corresponded to three primitive anthropoid stocks, linked to the three kinds of anthropoid apes. Whether the new view be correct or not, and there is something to be said in its favour, there can be no reasonable doubt now as to the close affinity which those creatures have to ourselves and to one another.

When we first encounter remains of man or his close predecessor in the records of the rocks, he was a dweller in holes and caves of the earth. He certainly did not make pots of any kind, or at least he has left no such remains. Probably he had no such companions even as the domestic dog or cat, no cattle, not at first any kind of grain crop. He lived on roots and fruits, hunted, and fished. Those early people have often been called Troglodytes, from the Greek τρώγλη, a cave.

Professor Keith, the learned curator of the museum of the Royal College of Surgeons, has advanced the theory that about the middle of the Miocene Age a group of creatures existed, having affinities to man as he now is, which group the professor names Proto-troglodytes. From these sprung three classes of Troglodytes, namely:

The Gorilla;
The Chimpanzee;
Man.

Some eighty-seven anatomical features are said to be possessed by the gorilla in common with man only, while the chimpanzee has ninety-eight such features as belong to man. The gorilla has the best and biggest teeth, and in this respect progressive deterioration went on through the orang-utan and the chimpanzee to man. According to the estimate of Professor Keith, there are not in the whole world, at present, more than 100,000 chimpanzee, and some 10,000 gorillas.

The subject of twins is likely in future to be very interesting in relation to the resemblance of their finger-patterns. The distinction is now made of twins proceeding from one zygote or fertilized ovum, and twins proceeding each from different fertilized ova. In the first case, it is supposed that the twins are necessarily of the same sex, while in the other, each twin child may be of the sex determined by the fertilized ovum from which it sprung. Clearly, in the latter case it might often happen that both twins might be male, or both female.

Dr. Berry Hart quotes from the records of another observer (Wilder) in which there was a pair of "identical" twins, in whom the similarity was complete even to the finger-prints. [*Brit. Med. Jour.*, July 29th, 1911, p. 215.] I have found in the same family male and female with *resembling* finger-prints, but none which could be called identical, but opportunities of comparing twins of the same sex do not often occur. While writing this chapter I examined twins of the same sex (female). Their finger-prints are very similar, but details diverge in many directions. The matter merits close attention. But how are we to determine that twins of the same sex are from one ovum, seeing that there might be a coincidence of twins of the same sex proceeding from separate ova? If their finger-prints are "identical," is that the main evidence? or do identity of features, colour of hair, voice, manners, and character, come up independently? If one questions the theory, the "identity" must be very complete indeed, to give it vraisemblance, for how often do we not find that children of the same parents, not twins, but born with many years intervening, show most striking resemblance? The alleged complete identity of finger-patterns, however, is a most interesting and novel point, and ought to receive close attention from parents and physicians. A curious fact about hereditary resemblance is this, which I have frequently observed. A child resembles, say, a mother as a rule, but at some emotional, angry, or vexed moment, lines are marked in the face by muscular movements which bring out like a mask a striking likeness, say, of the father, or of some other progenitor. Besides this, a child at different stages may resemble in succession different near relatives, and in a very striking degree resemble them. But with regard to finger-patterns there is no such variability. Even a month or two before a child is born its little heraldic crest begins to be firmly fixed for each finger, as it is to be throughout life.

The disease called Acromegaly, or giant growth, involves great expansion of the ridges and furrows, but no case of actual change of patterns has been observed as yet. The attention of medical men should be given to this affection in regard to modification of linear arrangement.

The likeness or divergence of finger-patterns in neighbouring supernumerary fingers and toes might yield interesting results if carefully recorded. Extra fingers are commoner than extra toes. The webbing of fingers, as in the chimpanzee, might also be noticed, and any association with retrograde patterns, in the fingers concerned.

The rapid growth of a literature of Criminology is partly the result of better methods of identification. It is unscientific to reason about the personal pecularities of all the Toms, Dicks, and Harrys, when Tom may be

Dick, or Dick Harry under a different alias. The criminologist can now use his prison statistics as to age, habits, and the like, with much greater confidence and precision. In an interesting, but somewhat reckless work on "Criminal Man," which summarizes the teaching of the eminent Italian authority on the anatomy and psychology of the criminal—of the Italian criminal at least—Cesare Lombroso, we are told (p. 20): "Long fingers are common to swindlers, thieves, sexual offenders, and pickpockets. The lines on the palmar surfaces of the finger-tips are often of a simple nature, as in the anthropoids." But they are not, necessarily, of a simple nature in the anthropoids, but often highly ornate and complex in their ramifications. In the lower monkeys they are much simpler, and Sir F. Galton thought it was so sometimes in the negro peoples. Indeed, one is not surprised to meet such simple lineation patterns now and again in cultivated people, without any criminal taint, or negro blood, or any anti-socialistic tendencies that can be easily detected. A cautious prison doctor in Glasgow, Dr. Devon, has written a clever book which gives much food for sober reflection. He seems to say that the criminal is not a kind of species by himself: "If those who come to prison for the first time were made the subject of examination, it would be found that they are principally remarkable for the absence of what the books call criminal characteristics." (p. 11.)

CHAPTER V

TECHNIQUE OF PRINTING AND SCRUTINIZING FINGER-PATTERNS

THERE are important points connected with the printing of finger-patterns, especially for legal investigation, which come now to be considered. A human finger, as we have seen, is not, for printing purposes, just like a lithographic stone, a box-wood engraving, or a plate of zinc, steel, or copper. In ordinary printing, especially of high-class and delicate engravings, the quality and fluency of ink, the smoothness of surface and hygrometric conditions of paper—due sometimes to local atmosphere, and sometimes to climate generally—the skill of workmen, all the conditions co-operate in producing variations, slight it may be, but noticeable in the results obtained. In the case of finger-prints we might also have to consider the willingness or unwillingness of the subject having his finger-prints officially taken. A finger—even that of a dead person—is compressible, while retaining on the whole the pattern of its furrows and ridges, and hence under fairly similar conditions, the printed products may be somewhat different in appearance. The same fact would apply, no doubt, also to impressions taken from an indiarubber stamp, made, we shall suppose, for stamping purposes in regard to documents, in imitation of a particular finger-print pattern. Greater compression tends to flatten out the ridges and to narrow the intervening grooves, while it may also tend, especially when associated with over-inking, to obliterate some of the characteristic ramifications of the pattern. But, again, the finger of a living person is usually in a state of physiological activity. It swells or shrinks, drying up or exuding moisture from its many pores, which facts, however minute and insignificant they may appear to the uninstructed, to the trained dactylographer they leave a most interesting and significant record behind.

Examine carefully a ridge which has been printed—and, if possible, photographically enlarged—at various periods not long apart, and the pores with which it is dotted will be found, while retaining their relative positions, to vary somewhat in their degree of patency. A single ridge might be compared to a naval cruiser, the numerous funnels of which are not all belching forth smoke at the same time, but one is almost smokeless while its neighbour is quite active. Those pores which have been copiously emitting sweat are seen, when imprinted, to be larger than those that were inactive. An imaginary case was once suggested to me as a final blow to finger-print identification. A certain Mr. William Sykes is officially known to be recruiting his valuable health at one of His Majesty's sanatoriums for people of his profession. That celebrated artist's "thumb"-print, however, has been found liberally spotted all over the scene of some tragic area of crime. What is to be said? Well, the prodigality of display of the well-known sign-manual, in circumstances when gloves are almost invariably now worn by experts, might well arouse suspicion in itself, but it would easily be found in such a case that the pattern had been prodigally repeated with too great fidelity in the matter of sweat-pores, which, in the case of an active burglar, who is a sober, hard-working fellow in spite of his faults, would vary with each successive imprint, in a way that no manufacturer of bogus "thumb"-prints could easily follow.

The fact that a finger—a clean finger—is naturally, to some slight extent, greasy, partly from sebaceous secretion, enables the expert dactylographer by various chemical and mechanical means to obtain a pretty clear vision, even in minute detail, of what before had been quite invisible. A mere accidental smudge from a slightly oily palm or finger, if imprinted on glass, japanned tin, varnished or polished wood, etc., may have its invisible lineations brought out by dusting gently upon it some light powder of appropriate colour. Dr. René Forgeot, in 1891, first called attention to this method of bringing out latent imprints, and my friend, Dr. Garson, of this country, gave it further developments.

In my *Guide* I have mentioned some of my own results with modifications of these methods.

On a pane of glass which a malign finger is suspected to have touched, a fine black powder gives vivid and beautiful results, the sooty matter clinging to and revealing the oily surface of the lineations in very full detail. In my article in *Nature* of 1880 a sooty imprint is shown to have helped an innocent man to establish his innocence, but in this case the imprint was quite direct. The powder should be gently blown over, or dusted lightly on to the greasy impression, with a soft camel hair brush which is perfectly clean and dry. Care should be taken not to breathe on the glass, or a damp, smeary effect may result. I have not found sable brushes act so well as those made of camel hair, a fact which their structure under the microscope helps to explain. (See frontispiece.)

The best treatment of a greasy smudge on a dark ground, say the surface of a japanned cash-box, marble slab, school slate, or enamelled door panel, is carefully to dust over the object with a fine white powder, such as the ordinary tooth-powder of the chemists, or still better, as I find, with the light carbonate of magnesia. In one sense this may be said to yield a *negative* print, but an important qualification arises. The patterns now in white are the ridges which before were black, while the furrows remain dark as at first. In a smoked glass print the white ridges have not imparted something to the glass, but have simply removed the carbonaceous deposit previously there. Practically, however, the whitened ridges have the quality of a negative imprint, as previously described.*

Greasy finger-marks may also be acted on chemically, so as to bring out details by the application of osmic acid. If there is any olein or oleic acid in the mark, as there generally is in human finger-marks, the acid deepens the tone of the almost invisible lines into a brownish hue, revealing all their richness of detail. I have succeeded in etching finger-marks of this kind on glass by means of hydro-fluoric acid. They remain quite indelible in all their details so long as the glass itself endures. The patterns thus etched can be very well brought into view by painting a dark background on the reverse, or pasting dark paper behind. There is a clear layer of the skin in both palms and soles, the

* See *Guide to Finger-Print Identification* (fig. 12)

fat of which is eleidin. That particular kind of fat does not stain with osmic acid in the usual way. The sweat of palms and soles is not supposed to contain any fat at all, but there would seem to be some faint trace of it in sweat. The greasy surface of the skin as a rule comes from the sebaceous glands, as previously described. When clean palms leave a greasy smear, as they often do, I think the greasiness must generally come by transmission from other parts of the body, or from contact with foreign greasy substances, which are common enough.

For those who wish to study dactylography, the apparatus is neither complicated nor expensive. A good pair of compasses, a botanical lens, a school slate or tin plate or porcelain tile, a small pot of fine printer's ink, and an ink-roller or photographer's "squeegee" will suffice for most purposes. For the expert who must make fine measurements of enlarged photographs, and perhaps defend them under keen forensic criticism, one or two instruments are required, presently to be described.

The ink may be daubed evenly and thinly on the slate, tile or plate, but it is better to use a small printer's roller for the purpose. Avoid all fluff, hairs, or grit, which thoroughly spoil any print. The roller should always be scrupulously cleaned before laying aside, and it is well to provide a tin case for its reception. The remaining stock of ink should be carefully levelled a-top, and covered with a drop or two of linseed or other oil, which will preserve it in good and workable condition for a long time. Reeve's Artists' Depôts, Ltd., 53 Moorgate Street, London, supply an excellent quality of ink for this purpose, in flexible tubes, at sixpence each, and the same firm can generally provide the rollers or squeegees used by photographers, which serve very well. In an emergency I have made serviceable ink with burnt cork, lamp soot, even shoe-blacking, using a good smooth and even cork as a roller. Wax casts, which should occasionally be made for study, can be made with the sheets of wax used greatly, at one time, for the making of artificial flowers. Excellent casts can also be made with putty, gutta-percha, sealing-wax, or hard paraffin, such as is used to encase the modern candle. Very excellent imprints of this kind have been left by burglars on candles they have used.

Some useful practical hints as to how finger-prints may be photographed and enlarged for police purposes are supplied by Inspectors Stedman and Collins, in an official work by Sir E. R. Henry, *Classification and Uses of Finger-Prints*; and others occur in *Daktyloskopie*, published in Vienna. Finger-marks on plated articles, when placed squarely with the camera in a strong side light, will appear light on a dark ground. The instructions in such a case are: "Focus sharply. Should, however, the mark be too faint to be clearly seen on the focussing screen, a piece of printed paper can be placed around the mark to focus by, but this should be removed before exposing the plate, otherwise halation will set in and obscure some of the lines in the finger-mark." The plate done in this way gives a negative result, so that a transparency must be made and used so as to convert that into a positive print.

The fingers and thumbs may each be printed separately. For identification the serial order of fingers must be retained on the record. The official method in England is to print four fingers of each hand simultaneously, adding the right and left thumb to each respective section of the register. In addition, each thumb and finger is imprinted by rolling it slightly, which gives an enlarged area for the display of the more important linear elements in each finger pattern.

The prisoner signs this sheet, and also adhibits an imprint from his right forefinger under the signature.

The highly-glazed papers now so much used for half-tone photographic reproductions are not, in my experience, particularly good for ordinary impressions. The surface of any paper used should be fairly smooth, the texture firm, tough (not brittle), durable, and the colour white, as photographs for enlargement as judicial exhibits may be required.

Great care is now taken officially to secure the correct order of fingers, as on that the validity of the method depends, and the whole utility of the classification.

Inspectors Stedman and Collins, in the work just quoted, state that when finger-prints are required to be produced as evidence in a court of justice, "they are first enlarged 5 diameters direct with an enlarging camera. The negatives are afterwards placed in an electric light enlarging lantern, with which it is possible to obtain a photographic enlargement of a finger-print 36 inches square, such a photograph being as large as is ever likely to be required."

In my *Guide to Finger-Print Identification* (p. 62) I have advocated uniform enlargement of all such exhibits on the decimal or metric system, and hope that international agreement on this point may be secured. Apart from criminal services its scientific utility would ultimately be very great. The objection that an English jury would dislike being confronted with the technicalities of a foreign and "mathematical" system is very easily met. An English jury—and no jury in the world is fairer or clearer-headed—would only, in any case, have to compare two figures *similarly enlarged*, one being that of the accused person's fingers, taken while in custody, and the other, either a similar official record of another date, or a smudgy mark from some blotting-pad, window-pane, drinking-glass, bottle, or the like. The two exhibits, paired for comparison, would have been enlarged exactly on the same scale, whatever that scale might have been. For purposes of judicial comparison, therefore, English terms and English instruments might be used throughout, and no inconvenience could be felt by the most insularly prejudiced jury that could possibly be got together.

When a photographic enlargement has been made, it is necessary to be able readily to test its conformity with the enlargement to be compared with it, or if there be not strict agreement, to allow for and calculate the admitted discrepancy. This may easily be done by an application of the "rule of three."

It may be necessary to test the concurrence of curved lines in two exhibits similarly enlarged. At one time I used strips of plumber's lead, placed edgeways on the curved lines to be compared. They could be flexed so as to show the various sinuosities, however complex, but leaden tapes cannot readily be made to retain the form imparted to them. Copper wire I found to be stiffer, but it readily warps off the plane. An excellent way is

MALE.

H.C.R. No. ____________

Name ____________ | **Classification No.** $\frac{26 \quad 0}{2 \quad 00}$ 11

Aliases ____________

Prison ____________

Prison Reg. No. ____________

RIGHT HAND.

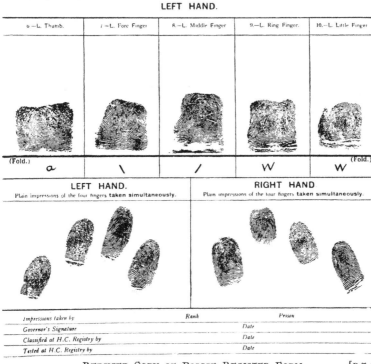

1.—Right Thumb.	2.—R. Fore Finger	3. R. Middle Finger.	4.—R. Ring Finger.	5.—R. Little Finger.

(Fold.) \	C.P. - ? \	/	W	\ (Fold.)

Impressions to be so taken that the flexure of the last joint shall be immediately above the black line marked (Fold). If the impression of any digit be defective a second print may be taken in the vacant space above it.

When a finger is missing or so injured that the impression cannot be obtained, or is deformed and yields a bad print, the fact should be noted under *Remarks*.

LEFT HAND.

6.—L. Thumb.	7.—L. Fore Finger	8.—L. Middle Finger	9.—L. Ring Finger.	10.—L. Little Finger

(Fold.) a	\	/	W	W (Fold.)

LEFT HAND.	RIGHT HAND
Plain impressions of the four fingers **taken simultaneously.**	Plain impressions of the four fingers **taken simultaneously.**

Impressions taken by ____ *Rank* ____ *Prison* ____

Governor's Signature ____ *Date* ____

Classified at H.C. Registry by ____ *Date* ____

Tested at H.C. Registry by ____ *Date* ____

REDUCED COPY OF POLICE REGISTER FORM [P.T.O.

Right forefinger print.
To be impressed
immediately after
signature is written.

Prisoner's Signature ____________________

NAME	
Year of Birth	Complexion
Hair	Eyes
Height ft.	in.
Last Conviction. *Sentenced at	
,, on	
,, to	
,, *for	
*Give offence in full, and if remanded only, substitute "Remanded" for "Sentenced."	

REMARKS.

[Opposite p. 69

to draw on transparent paper a line corresponding to the curved line seen underneath. The transparency is then transferred and adjusted to the other enlargement, the curves of which should be seen to be congruent. The instrument called "flexible curves" which is used by engineers and mechanical draughtsmen I at last tried, and found it to be exceedingly serviceable for such comparisons. The pattern "B," self-clamping, 12-inch size, is for most cases the most suitable. Other patterns are made also, in sizes of 9 and 18 inches. The "B" pattern has a flexible steel strip, like the lead tape just mentioned. After the curve or series of sinuosities has been adjusted to correctly, the shape is rigidly retained by means of a

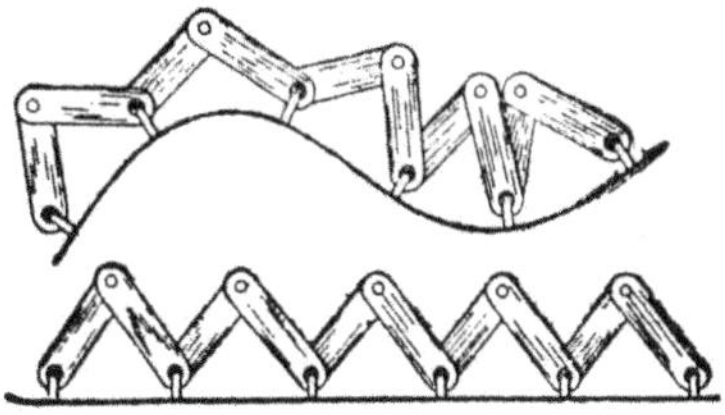

FLEXIBLE CURVES.

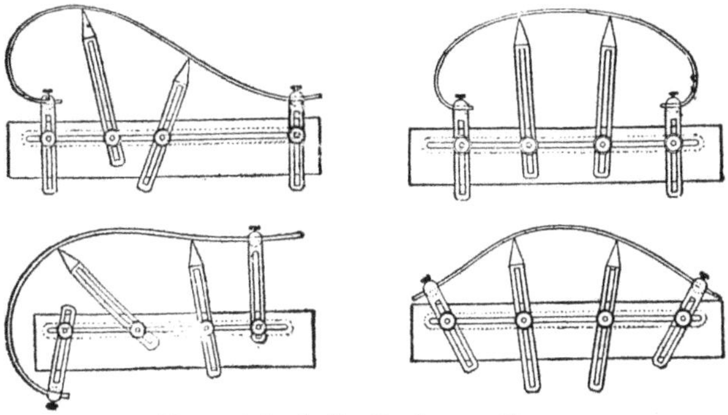

HARLING'S J. R. B. CURVE RULES.

stiff-hinged link-work arrangement attached by tabs. The strip of steel should not be pressed down between two tabs, and when bending or straightening out the instrument one should do so bit by bit, beginning at one end and continuing onwards from there. This useful self-clamping instrument used to be supplied by Mr. Wm. Brooks, scientific instrument maker, 33 Fitzroy Street, Tottenham Court Road, London. Another instrument of this kind, the "Curve Rule" is sold by Mr. W. Harling, 47 Finsbury Pavement, E.C., and is figured here.

In dealing with such *approximate* curves as one finds among the lineations of finger-prints, one is not supposed to apply strictly mathematical principles. The lines, for example, have breadth, but not quite invariable breadth. We must, therefore, avoid treating them, as a beginner fresh from the schools is apt to do, as ideal concepts. The simpler terms, however, as used by a teacher of drawing, with the provisos already hinted at, will serve very well to guide one's efforts, or to explain one's own conceptions before a magistrate or a jury.

Besides the congruity of the curves, one has further to test the single lineations, their junctions, number, and character. An excellent way to envisage these is to make alternate linings with blue and red pencil, to represent them as they seem. To do this effectively one may single out a special measured square, or circle, or parallelogram, of the enlarged figure. Proceed then, quite ignoring, if need be, all great curvatures, to consider the lines as simple curved or straight lines, and analyse them into composing elements, like twigs of a tree or the characteristics of a runic alphabet. The result will be, perhaps, like the figure on the next page.

It will now be quite easy to orient, or place correctly in space, the corresponding part of the other print—if it really does correspond—and a similar "rune" should result. One may afterwards follow out each recognized lineation into further complexities or joinings, as you might trace out a railway line with its various junctions in a map.

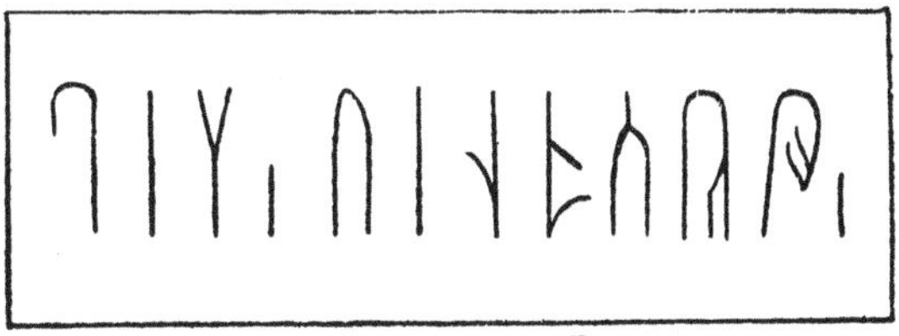

DIAGRAMMATIC ANALYSIS OF LINEATIONS IN A RESTRICTED SECTION.

A photographic enlargement, meant for forensic use, ought not to be marked or soiled in any way, but dots of coloured chalk or ink might be placed along the margins to denote where imaginary ruled lines might begin or end. One might also use glazed tissue paper, ruled in squares, or with eccentric circles like the mileage lines in a map of London. By the use of these placed over the figure one might verify particular coincidences or demonstrate discrepancies.

When the skin-pattern is impressed upon soft sealing-wax, clay, putty, and so on, the *relievo* image produced is different in this way from an ordinary ink-printed pattern. The convex ridges are now concave furrows, while the hollows are changed into heights.

In both kinds of impressions a reverse or *mirror* pattern is produced, a matter of some practical importance. This effect may, or may not again be reversed in the photographic process. It is not impossible, in such circumstances, that a suspect's finger might be confused with a resembling "mirror" pattern, which was really not his own.

I have thought that the word *verso*, used technically for the reverse of a coin or medal, might be usefully employed in dactylography for the reverse or mirror image of a finger-pattern when printed. A technical word for the indented impression made by a finger on wax and the like is also wanted. Now geologists use *-lite* as a terminal to express the impression or cavity which had been formed in a rock, when soft, by the impressed body of an organism. Hence the word *dactylolite* might be used to denote an indented impression of a finger.

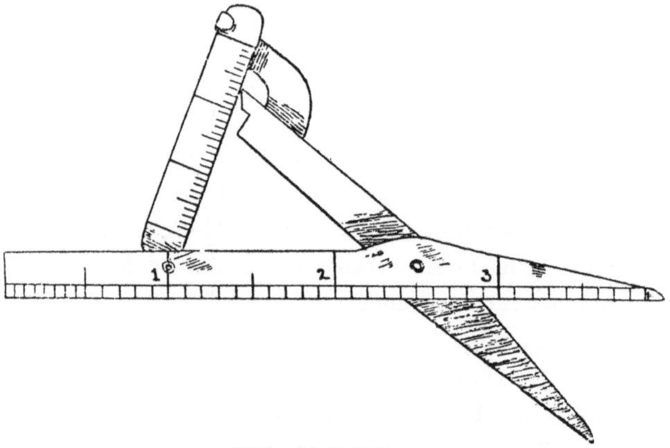

KEW MICROMETER.

In making measurements of exhibits, the Kew micrometer devised by Sir Joseph Hooker is of much service. It is figured here, and has the useful quality of rendering measurements at the same time in both the English and decimal systems.

For the method of encircling suspect smudges, either before or after enlargement, and measuring from one fixed centre by the Kew micrometer or ordinary compasses, I have devised a disc of glass such as is used in microscope slides, and about the size of half-a-crown. In the centre is a conical pit into which one leg of the compass rests. Precise centring is thus obtained without the slightest risk of damaging the photographic or other exhibit by the sharp point of the compasses, which have, at the same time, free swing. These were prepared for me by Mr. Franks, optician, Stoke-on-Trent, and cost very little.

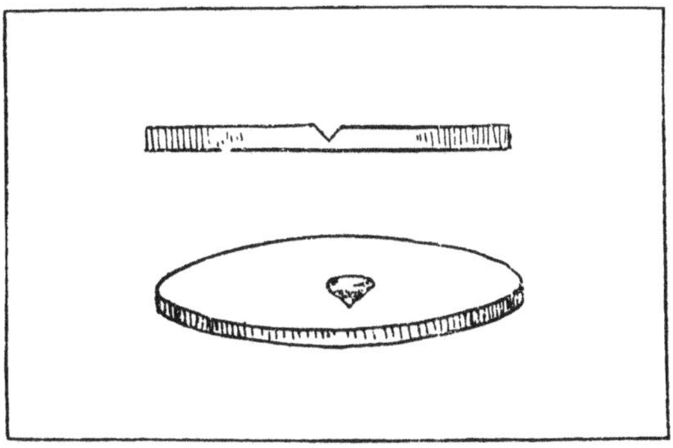

GLASS DISC CENTRED (enlarged).

In all measurements close to a fork or junction, as in the crook of the letter Y, care must be taken in counting the lines below or above the fork. Ambiguity readily arises, with a train of resulting discrepancies. Other ambiguities also occur which require mention in a word or two. In deciphering an ancient manuscript blurred, mouldy, mayhap worm-eaten, doubts may arise as to which of two or three possible words or letters may have been intended. One looks for some rationality in the author's writing, but in finger-prints there can be no such help. In manuscripts the problem may not directly be as to a word, but only as to a letter, but that single letter, read differently, may change the tenor of a passage. Is C to be read as C or as G or as O? Is E to be read as E or as B? So Fork is liable to be read as Pork.

Now, a very similar difficulty frequently occurs in reading a blurred finger-print, and such evidence should be scrutinized with the greatest vigilance, and all really doubtful cases should be discarded as useless in evidence. While the obscurity is sometimes merely due to defective printing, there are several patterns of frequent occurrence which are liable to be read variably. This was discussed at some length in chapter iii. of the *Guide*. There is a tendency so to view blots or blurs in such a case, that the cloudy spots become a weasel or even a whale. In Japan there are artists' wine-parties, where a common game is to make an accidental splash of ink or colour, which is passed on to the next guest, who in turn converts it by one or more strokes of the brush into a figure of some character. Some years ago, I gave to a young men's meeting a lecture on Ghosts, in which I showed a collection of ink-splashes produced without design, some of which were quite strikingly artistic in their suggestive impressionism. Hence the importance of clear printing, vigilant scrutiny of exhibits to be compared, and the attention of a well-informed judge and intelligent jury.

In certain circumstances, when a suspected person has been arrested abroad or at a distance, it may be desirable to compare his fresh finger-prints broadly with that of some well-known criminal whose register has been long in the hands of the police. This want led me to suggest, in 1905, that photo-telegraphy, in one of its forms, might be brought into use. Many improvements have been made since then, and it is now, I think, quite feasible to secure and transmit to a great distance outline lineations quite good enough for use at a preliminary enquiry, previous to a remand or committal.

CHAPTER VI

PERSISTENCE OF PATTERNS

A HUMAN finger, in ordinary circumstances, may preserve, unimpaired, not only its general pattern of lineations, sometimes very intricate, during its owner's lifetime, but the minutest details also may be discerned after thirty or forty years, quite unchanged as elements of a pattern, and very likely for a longer period, though scientific observation has not extended much beyond that limit. Long immersion, after death, in water, till the skin is quite sodden, does not readily destroy, does not even greatly obscure, the lineations for the purpose of comparison with earlier printed records of them, and one can still read into finger-print type, so to speak, the lineations of an Egyptian mummy.

When first I ventured to call the attention of the scientific world to the patterns of finger-prints in 1879 or 1880, I suggested that the ancient mummies of Egypt might possibly be found to have retained those features sufficiently to be studied. I had no opportunity of obtaining access to such remains in order to test the point, but on returning to England I found that anticipation to be amply justified, as anyone may verify by a visit to the British Museum. The skin of a mummy is contracted, hard, and wrinkled, but one may trace the lineations through all their loops, joinings, ramifications and whorls, with great distinctness. So that it follows, did an Egyptian register of finger-prints exist, we might unearth the names and titles or deeds of some of those men who lived several thousands of years ago.

There is nothing, so far as has yet been observed, to mark their race out as essentially different from our own, nor do any ancient finger-prints look unlike those of present-day people's.

The ridges on toes and fingers are visible in children born prematurely, even at a very early period, as I have observed in the practice of my profession, and as soon as the lineations are at all discernible they are of human type. So far as has yet been observed, we do not find that the growing human embryo repeats a history of finger-patterns, beginning at an earlier and lowlier biological stage, as is sometimes contended to be the case in regard to some other organic structures undergoing development.

The efforts I first made to investigate the problem of permanence were chiefly directed to the earlier periods of life, as presenting the greatest likelihood of variation in patterns during rapid growth. A large number of Japanese children, and also some thirty-five or more children of European parentage, in ages from five to ten, were minutely examined time after time during a period of two years—some of them again at longer intervals—without a single variation being detected. The lines and patterns in the fingers of growing children broaden out as the infant grows, but the ideal form—so to speak—of the pattern itself, retains full sway. To grasp this conception clearly is almost the whole science of finger-print identification.

During that period, some of those children suffered severely from scarlet fever, which, as a new disease, took a severe form in Japan, and the desquamation, or skin-peeling, was unusually severe, so that in those cases the test was a severe one. On several occasions I have called attention to the possibility of severe desquamation being followed by some change of patterns, and I still think this subject merits the attention of medical men, but no actual fact illustrating the apparent danger has yet been brought under notice. This may, however, be simply the result of a high degree of inattention to a subject which medical men do not seem to have interested themselves in until very recently. In acromegaly, a disease in which the fingers take on gigantic features, one might expect to find a very notable change of patterns, perhaps the addition of fresh lineations, but after some attempts to collect information not one single example of the kind has yet reached me.

Besides testing growing children in the manner I have stated, many Japanese medical students between the ages of twenty and thirty were made use of in this way. The ridges were carefully shaved by razors, or smoothed away by sand-paper, emery dust, or pumice stone, so that no distinct patterns could be traced. The same tests were applied to my own fingers and to those of one or two medical friends who were quite sceptical as to the continuity of the patterns. Many of the patients at the hospital, or out-door dispensary, were also induced to submit, but not a single instance of variation in the patterns was ever brought to light. My own finger-prints have not varied since that date, a period of fully thirty years. However smooth the surface had been made, the old design came up again with perfect fidelity, yielding exactly the same imprints as before, subject only to those very minor variations already described in a previous chapter, to which even engravings are subject. Up to the period of my final return to England in 1887, a period of nearly nine years, enthusiastic and vigilant observation of this point gave me complete confidence in the permanence of finger-print patterns as a basis of personal indentification. With the exception of acromegaly and skin-peeling after acute fevers, I can conceive of no biological reason why changes might be anticipated in those patterns, and up to the present no evidence has reached me that even those conditions do effect pattern changes. In old age the ridges shrink somewhat, and wrinkles here and there betray the drying up of tissues, which facts are revealed in printed impressions by fine white lines, often cutting across the lineations, not unlike those which occur in box-wood engravings, where hair-like lines betray some cleavage of the wood. In such a case the value of the pattern is not affected as a proof of identity. One may go beyond that, and say that, if after a lapse of forty years or so the old pattern is now crossed by wrinkles which were not there in youth, the two prints are from the same individual.

Other observers—Sir Francis Galton, Sir William Herschel, and the police of this and other countries—have accumulated a vast store of conclusive evidence on this point.

We are now amply justified in assuming that, for all practical purposes of identification, the patterns on human fingers are, throughout life, persistent and unchangeable. Such slight and transient changes—not due to mere variations of pressure, inking, and the like, as they usually are—are no more likely to invalidate an identification than a new freckle or pimple on a man's face would make him unrecognizable by his intimate friends.

Dr. J. G. Garson, in an article in the *Daily Express* of July 20th, 1905, writing on this subject, which he has carefully studied, said :—

> "It is now a well ascertained fact that every person bears on his fingers as certain proof of his identity as he does on his face. The latter is, however, that part of his anatomy by which he is most readily identified by the world at large, though to his intimate friends other particulars about him may characterise him equally strongly. By means of the eye, the *tout ensemble* of the countenance is registered upon the mind, generally regardless of details respecting the actual form of each particular feature—in short, a person is recognized and identified by exactly the same psychological process as a printed or written word is read without first spelling it."

It must be clear to any student of the subject that *persistence of patterns* must become the basis of identification in this way, and that persistence is now as firmly established as anything can be as to living creatures.

Sir Edward Henry, in his *Finger-Prints*, says (p. 17, 3rd edition) : "Impressions being required for permanent record, their utility must, in great measure, be contingent upon the persistence through long periods of time, of the general form of the pattern and of the details of the ridges constituting it." No such stability has yet been shown to exist in regard to any other part of the body. The bones change very greatly, not only in size, but in shape, texture, and mechanical conditions through life. Even the ordinary features and expression of a human being by no means can be said to remain uniform. One sees a friend during many short intervals, and is not finely observant of minute changes that in a decade or two amount collectively to an almost complete transformation of the man's whole face and figure. The photographic system of identification, although serving a purpose now and then, was found, therefore, to be untrustworthy.

My revered teacher, Lord Lister, noted the slow migrations of the pigmentary particles that make the web-like patterns on a frog's foot. I have observed similar but still slower changes in ordinary freckles on a human hand. The white spots of leucoderma—a skin-disease that used to be confused with leprosy, from which it entirely differs—are often bounded with dark borders, into which the pigment particles have migrated from the white spots. A negro's skin sometimes becomes white where a fly-blister has been applied, as a fair-skinned person is often marked with a dark patch after a similar application. The pigment particles move to and fro like living things, though very slowly, and the marks they collectively make on a living body are not fixed and stable. Again, we have seen that the police used to record the position of wens, tumours, tattoo marks and the like. But tumours are now often removed through the line of natural creases, or wrinkles, leaving very faint traces, if any, behind.

An official in Japan had a large wen on his forehead, which disfigured him greatly. He was getting elderly, and told me, when friends brought him, that he would as soon have the wen as a scar. I got him to consent to have it removed through the natural wrinkle in the forehead, after which it left no visible trace at all.

A curious case was that of a man whose back and shoulders were adorned by a large collection of a certain kind of tumour varying from the size of a chestnut to that of a hen's egg. They all disappeared, without the use of the knife, leaving no scar behind, and only a slight lowering and thinning of the skin.

Even scars, themselves, sometimes very unsightly ones, tone away to a large extent, till they cease to be at all conspicuous. The colour of the hair changes greatly in some people at the various stages of life. Certain diseases, too, such as malarious affections, the action of the sun, and certain employments, change the complexion in a very remarkable way.

What the pole-star used to be in navigation, finger-print patterns are now become for all serious purposes of practical identification.

CHAPTER VII

THE SYLLABIC CLASSIFICATION OF FINGER-PRINTS

HAVING secured some technical knowledge of how to print, and how to read old finger-prints correctly and with confidence when they turn up again in experience, we are faced now with the problem of how to classify and arrange them for secure preservation and prompt and easy reference, whatever may be our object.

In natural history, in biological facts generally, it is not always easy to define the objects of study strictly, so as to classify them in a practical way. Dealing, however, with printed finger-patterns which are no longer living and changing things, we can hope to secure some of the advantages of a mechanical method. Verworn, in his *General Physiology* (p. 71) says, very justly: "The fixing of sharp limits and definitions must contain, finally, a more or less arbitrary element, [that], indeed, all limits and definitions are only psychological helps towards knowledge." Bearing this principle in mind, then, what is the end or object we aim at in a system of finger-print classification?

The objects of identifying a person with some one who has had a name and left a history are of various kinds, as criminal, civil, military, naval, medical, legal, scientific, and insurance purposes. Now, in regard to the use of finger-prints for so many ends in view, a difficulty presents itself. It occurred to me at the outset of my studies, that if the system were to prove trustworthy and useful, even in a minor degree, immense numbers of people in civil life, in army, navy, and mercantile services, or under criminal conviction, would require to have their prints correctly classified, indexed, and arranged for easy reference. How could it be possible in so vast a collection or series of collections to find the one single record wanted? To ransack—unaided by a scientific method of classification—the register of an army containing some 500,000 soldiers would involve the search of a much larger number of cards or sheets than 500,000, according to the duration of regular service, and other possible conditions. To do this would obviously be quite as hopeless and futile a task as groping for a lost needle in a huge hay-field. The problem was to find a system which would facilitate the search in a *high degree.* Any mere slight assistance would still leave the essential problem unsolved. Now, we might have found in finger-prints mere variety without persistence, or mere persistence without initial variety, and in either case the study could yield little practical result. Again, mere diversity, however persistent, without some elements of underlying resemblance, would not have yielded a basis for such a methodic arrangement as was obviously required.

Much aid came to me from the first, as I have already hinted, from five years' daily laborious experience in sorting and comparing analogous but artificial patterns in the now obsolete Paisley shawl trade, but in the case now in view colour did not come in as an aid to arrangement. This problem, moreover, was not one of those the poet derides as of mere "gold or clay," but as I saw, it concerned itself with human lives, and was a task, indeed, that might awaken in the dullest mind a keen sense of moral responsibility in proposing its general use as a new and quite trustworthy method of criminal and other modes of identification. The expert in charge might suddenly be called upon after a little expansion of the system to prove the identity of some evil-doer out of many thousands of possible persons, or to subject a suspected person, on the evidence of a few smudgy streaks of ink or blood, to life-long servitude, or to the irremediable doom of a shameful death. In my own case, at this early stage, the mere possibility of a single serious false identification by a method as yet untried became really terrible to contemplate. After closer study, a clear path began to open through the tangled jungle.

Some familiarity with the equipment of a Far-Eastern printing-press had been afforded me while editing *The Chrysanthemum*, a monthly magazine published in Tokyo, and devoted to the discussion of Japanese topics of literary, scientific, or antiquarian interest. There were some hundreds of thousands of different forms of type, all classified in so convenient a way that any compositor, by running about a little more actively than would be quite compatible with the grave dignity of an English printing establishment, could soon find the character in whatever form of fount he desired. The idea suggested itself then, that analogous qualities as a basis for classification of the finger-patterns might be revealed by a closer study of Chinese. I do not know Chinese—some years' close study has convinced me of that. However, each Chinese ideograph, for dictionary purposes, is supposed to be built up around an element called by western lexicographers its *key* or *radical*, and of these there are two hundred and twelve. You look for the radical in an unknown character, and then look for that radical in its serial place in the two hundred and twelve. It is a question then, as in finger-prints, of counting strokes, and if the strokes are alike in number in any two instances, of looking then as to how they are arranged. Two characters with the same number of pen-strokes under the same radical or key, may bear quite a different aspect.

A Chinese character is defined and limited, but a finger-print pattern often, or usually, trails off into indeterminate lineations of little value for classification purposes. Hence we seek in the latter to isolate for study the central part of the pattern, where the intricacy of the ramifications usually rises to a maximum. The space covered by the lineations that matter is not usually greater than, often not so wide as, the space occupied by the head of the Sovereign on an English postage stamp. Into this brief compass is compressed a world of significance. A courteous and intelligent young detective in Scotland Yard asked me (in 1886 or 1887, when I was advocating the adoption of finger-print identification), did I really propose to rest identification on features contained within so small a space? I answered him, in pointing to a railway map of London, to consider a net-work of junctions which I indicated, if he would not be justified in saying if that fragment, torn away from its context, were presented to him, that it was a portion of a map of London? After a little scrutiny, he admitted that was so. I had no difficulty in showing him then, that the condensed ramifications of a single finger-print within the very limited area proposed by me were much greater than that of the significant portion of the London map I had just pointed out to him.

In tracking a criminal by a single impression made by a finger, the lineations in so small a space would require to have been clearly imprinted, and to have what many finger-print patterns have not, some notable or significant characteristics about it. Then, when enlarged by photography into a picture of some thirty inches, the measurements from fixed points in the pattern should correspond with those of the person in custody, on suspicion, and the curves should be shown to concur in all their sinuosities. But, in comparing two official imprints of the ten fingers properly and clearly impressed, there should be no difficulty, the points of comparison being overwhelming.

In a possible collection of half-a-million or a million complete sets of finger-prints, can the one before me, of one Thomas Atkins, John Doe, or Richard Roe—under whatever alias—be promptly found if it is there, or, if not there, can its absence be conclusively determined? We have seen, I think, that if two such patterns are confronted, common-sense, and the use of fine measurements, will soon determine whether they be of the same original, or different. The problem, then, is to get this swift and sure confrontation effected.

This problem engaged my attention from the first, or at least not many months after I first began to attend to finger-patterns, and in 1880, when I proposed the printing and recording of the ten fingers of old criminals,

I had thought out the same method now outlined in this chapter. It would be impossible to compress all the details necessary to work out the matter officially, without producing a work as large, and perhaps as expensive, as a Chinese dictionary, of which the probabilities are that one or perhaps two copies might be sold.

I laid this matter in outline before Inspector Tunbridge, in his official capacity, in 1888, and again before the War Office Committee, at which an Under-Secretary of the Home Office was present, taking diligent notes. The system now in official use—an improvement made by Sir Edward R. Henry upon Sir F. Galton's very premature attempt (after a few years' study in old age) seems to work practically, and therefore I have no criticism to offer, further than to suggest, that if in our system of mercantile book-keeping we had retained the use of Roman numerals, fortunes might continue to be made or lost. I cannot think, however, that our merchants would now give up the Arabic notation for the more complex and clumsy one of ancient Italy. Nor is nature likely to resume her interest in the kangaroo and its future.

Science seeks simplicity, and the *Syllabic system*, now familiar to every one who uses a telegraphic code, is what I proposed for finger-print registers. In this I simply followed the method of transliterating Japanese and Chinese words into syllables of the Roman alphabet, a condition originally imposed by the old Japanese language itself, in which consonants do not occur singly, but are followed by vowels. Purkinje's first analysis of the finger-print patterns was not known to me, nor, I believe, to anyone in Europe or America, when I first wrote, although I often in those years suggested that he had probably written something on the subject. My first article in *Nature*, as sent up, contained a kind of analysis of patterns, with many types, named as whorls, ovals, deltas, loops, junctions, and the like. Some are referred to in the text, but the editor expressed his regret that he had not been able to insert the figures, and their lack made the references in my article obscure. We shall deal with a few of these elementary or typical figures presently. But, let us now come to the main aspect of the syllabic system, in contrast with that devised by Sir F. Galton, who looked upon it as merely ancillary to the anthropometric system of Mons. A. Bertillon, of the French police. Galton was supremely anxious to have his natural facts, his finger-print records, arranged precisely in similar parcels, so that one would not be excessively rich in records compared with its neighbour. Now, what does it matter to the keeper of records, or even to the tax-payer, whether one class of patterns is big or little ? The whole absurd complexity arising now, and increasing from year to year, grows out of this essential misapprehension from the first of the vital problems of finger-print classification. Advancing a stage for the moment, let us suppose that a rich register exists, arranged on the syllabic system. A type-writer, not necessarily a very intellectual creature, or a boy-clerk, is in the room, and has the call to find *A-bra-ca-da-bra*. I use here for convenience only five syllables, representing one hand. The sheets or cards (sheets have been found best by experience) are not separated in bundles except as to a convenient size. It does not take long to look along the shelves till *A-bra-* etc., is reached, and then the cabalistic word itself. It may prove that there are some ten sheets on the register under this syllabic title. These are transmitted, all in a few moments, to the expert keeper of the records. At a glance an expert eye like his perceives that, perhaps, seven out of the ten can have no possible relation to the case now being enquired into. Of the three, one is perhaps now in prison and cannot be the suspect. Of the two remaining forms, the details of the first two fingers compared may diverge completely in many ways, as determined by counting lines, measuring curves, and so on. I am sure this would be no fancy description, from the many tests I have applied. The whole strain of the recognition lies on the expert, as the strain of the primary classification of records had lain upon him at the time they were being made. Of course, more than one expert might be needed.

It will be noticed, perhaps, that the syllable *bra* occurs twice on the same hand register. It by no means follows that the finger-print represented by the second *bra* is very like that of the first one. In the same way, none of the patterns indicated by *bra* in the cards of similar syllabic index may much resemble the others, even broadly. The pattern simply is of a certain typical form with which *bra* is to be linked for registration purposes. The same word, so to speak, might be divided in a different syllabic way, thus :—

Ab-ra-cad-ab-ra ;

Ab-rac-ad-ab-ra ; and so on.

Hence the necessity of separating the syllables by hyphens.

The divergence of cards will be greater, of course, in

the case of a two-hand register, and even in one which comprehended, say, one million of complete sets there would be very few repetitions of the same arrangement of syllables.

One great advantage of the syllabic form is the help given to the memory in transferring the eye from one sheet to others which may be wanted. In the system now in use the symbols do not rivet themselves in the same way, and have a monotony that becomes very tiring.

A general view of the precise intention aimed at in the particular register must determine the extensiveness of the form the register is to compass. Are the numbers likely to be large ? Must the registers extend over long periods ? Are infants to be kept in view over adult life, if that is reached ? Many enquiries of this kind may have to be met before the exact form of the cards or sheets is determined. For such civil and social purposes as life insurances, signatures of deeds, benefit of friendly societies, and the like, a comparatively simple form of register and limited number of finger imprints might be all that would be required for an effective service. The number of cards would not be very great, and the probabilities of personation would likely be restricted to a few local residents whose finger-prints would not often be found even to approach coincidence in a slight degree. To serve such needs, an elementary form of classification would go a long way to overtake ordinary requirements, and would be easy of reference. Few of the difficulties involved in graver conditions of legal identification need be raised as an objection to the general use in banking and ordinary business of this new mode of identification.

In forming a system, even with a very wide range, the whole amount of possible complexity in finger-patterns need rarely be called upon, and could not conceivably be exhausted. I speak confidently on this point. The central part of the pattern used is generally very limited, and its area may be widened whenever an enlargement of the primary requirements may demand more complexity in the factors of identification. The ramifications will usually provide variety enough to satisfy the most avaricious register.

Some of the main conditions on which the problem of alphabetic arrangement of the index depends may now be set forth, before we proceed to consider how those conventional syllables are to be formed which indicate patterns.

1.—Distinction is not made between capital and lower-case letters. Simple letters are too soon exhausted in a register of any considerable size. It is obvious that syllables give a much greater variety. As far as possible, commensurate with the dimensions of the register, the syllables should be kept few, simple, compact, and pronounceable. The vowels have the Italian sound. No syllables should contain more than four letters at the utmost.

2.—When a doubt arises as to the proper syllabic reading of a finger-pattern, the earlier letters of the Roman alphabet have the precedence, thus *b* before *d*, *l* before *x*.

3.—Where the core of a pattern seems to contain two or more clusters of significant lineations, choose for the index syllable that on the right side of the pattern, or, if that is difficult to determine, next that which is highest in position. In such a case, reference to orientation or position refers to the usual or official pattern. In dealing with a smudge of unknown origin, the various possibilities may be tried, assuming relative order of position, as above.

4.—When spaces or figures, such as ovals or circles, are described as "*large*," that means wider than the space occupied by two average lineations in that finger-print.

5.—When a finger-pattern has been permanently defaced or obliterated by injury or disease, the missing mark may be denoted by an asterisk (*). If the finger itself is missing, by deformity or mutilation, the asterisk may be encircled with an O. A special compartment of the register might be kept for the reception of all such cases.

6.—Badly-printed or obscure patterns should be held in reserve under a special register classified according to probabilities, aided by cross indexing, and receiving special attention from the higher experts. Official patterns badly printed should at once be repeated, if possible, before confusion arises.

7.—Registers for naval or military, and banking, insurance, and general purposes, should be kept strictly free from any police supervision or control.

The syllables in my system, viewed as lexicographic elements, consist of the ordinary Roman vowels and consonants, the vowels being pronounced, as already said, as in the Italian language. I hold in reserve for additional official purposes a few additional characters, such as the Greek letter *delta* Δ. Those, however, need not be dealt with in the brief space now available, and would only be required, I believe, in pretty extensive registers. The functions of the conventionally fixed vowels may be better understood after we have sampled a few of the consonants.

As suggested to me by Sir Isaac Pitman's system of phonography, learned in student years, I arranged the consonants in co-related pairs, thus: *p*, *b*; *t*, *d*; *s*, *z*; *h*, *f*; *l*, *r*; *k*, *g*; *v*, *w*; *ch* (considered as a consonantal character), *j*; *m*, *n*.

I have already pointed out, in dealing with problematic smudges, the need of understanding patterns apart from their actual orientation, which, in an unknown person's case, may have to be assumed, an attitude which may be determined by official bias. This I have entered more fully upon in the *Guide to Finger-Print Identification.*

Holding this principle in view, then, let us now take some of the simpler elements of patterns in their very simplest forms, and first consider those grouped under the paired consonants.

Ch and J.

Each of these characters is taken to represent a hook with a short leg. **Ch** is considered as one consonant, and as **C** is not otherwise wanted, it might have been used alone but for its pronunciation being indefinite. If in the usual form of official imprint the hook, with its curve below, has its short leg facing to the left, thus, **J**, it is duly represented by the Roman letter of that shape. Observe that if you invert this character, or the type which represents it, thus ſ, it will still point the observer to the **J** part of the index, on getting the curve set right.

If the short leg of the figure points to the right it comes under **Ch**. If that happens to confront one in its inverted position it cannot be mistaken for a **J** figure, but must be looked for under **Ch**. In all cases the degree or direction of slope in the figures, with a few peculiar exceptions, is of no concern whatever, simplicity and directness of appeal being aimed at from the first.

B and **P**.

These consonants are used to denote a bow. **B** is the form of a simple bow with one lineation, or if two or more lineations blend into one, they are found on the *left* side when the convexity of the curve is upwards. **P** is such a bow, but strengthened, as it were, by one or more blended lineations on the *right* side, with the same position of the curve. A single line bow is never represented by **P**. If a bow with a plurality of blended lineations is inverted the reading is not at all affected.

T and **D**

represent pear-shaped, or battledore-like figures. **T** denotes such a figure free from attachment to environing lineations, while **D** stands for a similar figure fixed by its stem. Reverse the position of the figure or turn it upside down and its index quality is not affected.

K and **G**

represent spindle-like forms, like the above but with *two* (opposite) stems instead of one. When the figure is moored by one stem it is denoted by **K**; when fixed at both ends or free at both, by **G**. Position does not affect these figures.

V and **W**.

These letters stand for whorls or spirals, a kind of figure that often presents much difficulty in finger-print classification. **W** is a whorl in which, tracing its course from the centre outwards, the pen goes round as a clock-hand turns, or as one looking towards the south perceives the sun to cross the sky. V, on the other hand, is one which, traced in the same way (from within outwards), the pen goes like the clock-hand backwards, or *widdershins*. Alteration in position makes no practical difference whatever in the reading of those figures into their proper syllables for an index.

O and Q

Although O is a vowel and will be met with again under that class, it is paired in a kind of way with Q.

O denotes a *small* circle or oval, or opaque, round, or ovoid dot, *contained in the core of a pattern.*

Q denotes a *large* circle or oval, containing, usually within itself, other pattern elements of small dimensions.

A circle or ovoid is called *large* when it occupies a space wider than two average lineations of that finger-pattern in which it occurs. If any doubt exists, by the principle previously mentioned, the figure is referred to O as prior to Q in alphabetical sequence.

M and N

denote figures somewhat resembling mountain peaks, M signifying an outline like that of a typical volcanic peak, while N, though similar, ends in a rod-like form, as of a flag-staff on a mountain top. Invert either of those typical forms and they can be read as before.

A curved cliff-like form, like a wave with a curling crest, may be indicated by the Spanish ñ.

L and R

denote loops in which curvatures are apt to occur. L is a loop, the axis of which is straight, while R is one the axis of which is curved or crooked.

Note that if the legs of a loop widen out beyond the parallels, it is no longer a loop, but a bow or a mountain.

They may narrow again and yet remain loops till at last they coalesce, when the figure is transformed into a spindle or a battledore (**T**, **D** ; *or* **K**, **G**). If the bend is more than that of a right angle, it comes under a new definition, and has some qualities of the whorl or spiral, but is more complex. This need not be entered upon here.

S and Z

I have used these two consonants to indicate certain patterns of a sinuous, undulating, or zig-zag type, the sinuous or purely undulating figures coming under **S**, but under **Z** if there is at least one distinct angularity in the pattern.

X

This letter, long familiar to the student of algebra as the symbol of the undetermined, I have reserved for the inclusion of various nondescript and anomalous patterns. Those might become fairly numerous in an extensive register, and in such case there would, no doubt, be found a good basis for fresh sub-classification.

F and H

These two aspirates are made to do useful service, not unlike that of vowels, but not of sufficient interest to be noted in a work like this.

We have thus, with the use of consonants alone, built up a kind of osseous or skeletal system, and we have now but to add the vowels to make those dry bones speak. Let us now consider this element in the syllabic method.

A

This vowel indicates that the interior of a given loop, whorl, circle, or containing pattern of any kind, is empty or vacant. Dealing here only with the simpler conditions in which combinations of vowels and consonants are found, such a figure will be indexed as *Ra*, *La*, *Ta*, *Da*, as the dominant consonant may require. Such combinations as *ar*, *al*, *at*, *ad*, etc., may occur, but this would lead us into too many intricate ramifications for a work like the present.

If a pattern is very simple—consisting, for example, of almost parallel lines—it may be denoted by the letter **A** alone. There are such patterns, and they seem to be somewhat commoner among certain of the negro tribes. I have mentioned in a previous chapter such a pattern on the toe of a lady, and they are typical almost in some monkeys.

E

When we find in the interior of some loop, bow, or other pattern, a group of not less than three short detached lines, or dots, this is to be indicated by the use of **E** with the ruling consonant, as *te*, *re*, *me*, and so on.

I

stands for a simple detached line, or not more than two parallel lines, in the heart of an encircling pattern.

O

stands for a little oval or circle, or for a round or oval-shaped dot in a core. If the circle, oval, etc. is *large*, extending over a width occupied by two lineations, then it is treated as a consonantal form. [See also **Q**.]

U

indicates a fork with two or more prongs within a core, forking towards the bend of bow, loop, mountain, etc. A single prong or spur standing out like a twig is to be istinguished from a fork.

Y

is for a similar fork as described above, but turning its two or more prongs away from the concavity of its enclosing loop, bow, etc.

Besides the direct combination of simple vowels and consonants, which arrangement by itself gives great variety to the index registers, an immense number of syllables are formed by combinations of two or more consonants, while some few of the vowels are treated as long or short where the pattern needs further discrimination; as, for example :—

bra, spo, art, prīd, prĭd, nut, nŭt.

By this method the most extensive register is gripped *and needs no other index than its own essential structure.* If the sheets or cards are kept in their proper sequence, and it would require to be the duty of some one—not necessarily an expert—to see that the alphabetic syllables were kept in serial order, there should be no difficulty in finding the document sought for, if it is there at all.

In translating fresh finger-prints into syllabic form, one has to catch the ideal design, so to speak, in the pattern. The consonantal skeleton, in one of its duplicate forms, is then examined for its containing vowel, and the syllable is complete. The work can be done with amazing rapidity after one is familiar with the patterns, which soon appeal direct to the eye as the type does in a printed book.

Let us now look at a few examples tabulated to show how the system works in detail.

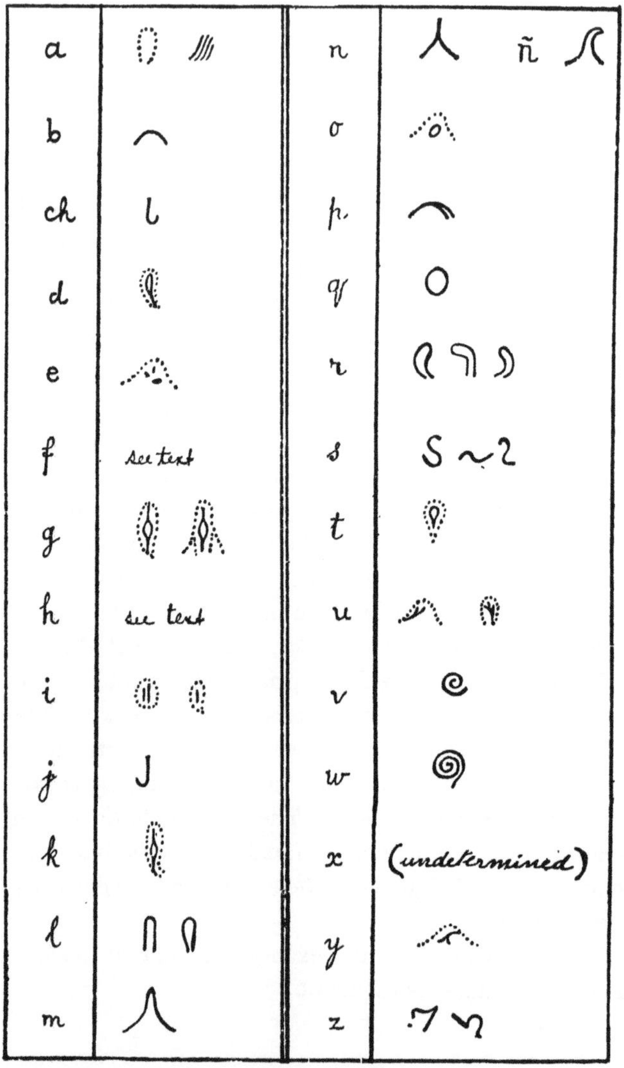

a
b
ch
d
e
f
see text
g
h
see text
i
j
k
l
m
n
ñ
o
p
q
r
s
t
u
v
w
x
(undetermined)
y
z

VOWELS AND CONSONANTS IN SYLLABIC CLASSIFICATION
with typical specimens of figure elements.

CHAPTER VIII

PRACTICAL RESULTS AND FUTURE PROSPECTS OF DACTYLOGRAPHY

TILL quite recently the method of identifying prisoners was that of personal recognition, often very admirably carried out. One may readily conceive that a criminal officer, a Bow Street runner of the old school, or a modern detective, might acquire great acuteness in perceiving points of individual character in face, form, gait, speech, and manner; and during the period of arrest, trial, and imprisonment there were many opportunities of observing notable offenders. Nor is such a power to be despised at the present time. How helpful a little point might even be under skilful disguise occurred to my own mind in this way. When I saw the great Henry Irving in the part of Mephistopheles in "Faust," a certain slight stiffness in the calves was assumed, by me, to be a very clever and subtle suggestion of the cloven hoofs which were supposed to aid the movements of that mediaeval personage. But the great actor walked other totally different parts in the same way, so that on the street, in any disguise, the notice of an acute detective might have been arrested. I am short-sighted, but can often recognize people at a distance too great to distinguish features, by some peculiarity of gait or gesture. In Taylor's *Manual of Medical Jurisprudence* [ed. of 1891, pp. 317, 318], there is a curious and interesting example of how recognition sometimes failed. The story is thus told :—

"A trial took place at the Old Bailey in 1834, in which a man was wrongly charged with being a convict, and with having unlawfully returned from transportation. The chief clerk of Bow Street produced a certificate, dated in 1817, of the conviction of a person, alleged to be the prisoner, under the name of Stuart. The governor of the gaol in which Stuart was confined believed the prisoner to be the person who was then in his custody. The guard of the hulks to which Stuart was consigned from the gaol swore most positively that the prisoner was the man. On the cross-examination of this witness, he admitted that the prisoner Stuart, who was in his custody in 1817, had a wen on his left hand ; and so well-marked was this that it formed part of his description in the books of the convict-hulk. The prisoner said his name was *Stipler* : he denied that he was the person named Stuart, but from the lapse of years he was unable to bring forward any evidence. The Recorder was proceeding to charge the jury, when the counsel for the defence requested to be permitted to put a question to an eminent surgeon, Carpue, who happened, accidentally, to be present in court. He deposed that it was impossible to *remove such a wen as had been described, without leaving a mark or cicatrix.* Both hands of the prisoner were examined, but no wen, nor any mark of a wen having been removed, was found. Upon this the jury acquitted the prisoner."

Charles Dickens, aided by the pencil of "Phiz," in *The Pickwick Papers*, gives us the power of seeing the process of "portrait taking," which was simply done by a group of runners and warders staring hard at the prisoner and noting his points.

In a Blue Book, *Identification of Habitual Criminals*, published in 1892, which contains the report of a Committee appointed by Mr. Asquith, who was then Home Secretary, we read that :—

> "The practice of the English police, though the details differ widely in different forces, is always dependent on personal recognition by police or prison officers. This is the means by which identity is *proved* in criminal courts; and, though its scope is extended by photography, and it is in some cases aided by such devices as the registers of distinctive marks, it also remains universally the basis of the methods by which identity is *discovered*."

The Register of Distinctive Marks, such as the wen in the case just mentioned, contained under nine divisions of the body those permanent scars from wounds, operations or burns, tattoo marks, moles, wens, warts, mother marks, etc., which might be expected to prove helpful in identification. Those registers were published annually, and distributed to all the different forces throughout the country. The system does not seem to have been very successful. For example, out of sixty-one enquiries, in twenty cases no information was obtained. As to the remaining forty-one cases, eight were incorrect, while of ten cases no ultimate intelligence reached the Registrar. The conclusion of the Committee is thus stated (p. 8) :—

> "It appears to us, therefore, that the comparative failure of these registers is due, not to any want of care in the way in which the work has been done, nor to the mode of classification, but rather to the inherent difficulty of devising any exhaustive classification of criminals on the basis of bodily marks alone, and also to the difficulty of using a register of criminals that is published at intervals and in a printed form."

Four years before this, as I have stated, I submitted to Inspector Tunbridge, deputed from Scotland Yard to meet me, an "exhaustive classification of criminals on the basis of bodily marks alone," but the chairman of that Committee, now Sir Charles E. Troup, told me himself, at the Home Office, that he had never heard anything of it. It is now, however, in use pretty well throughout the civilized world.

Some progress, nevertheless, was made. A card index was recommended, and greater definiteness in the description of the bodily marks was to be observed. A very notable change was also foreshadowed in the whole conception of the subject.

It is interesting now to read that "it was strongly represented to us by Chief-Inspector Neame and his officers, that there should be greater precision in the taking of descriptive marks, and that their distance from fixed points in the body should be measured and recorded." Science is measurement, and it is highly creditable to the English police that this demand was now to come from them.

Here is a specimen of the Register Form as applying to the Right Arm—one of the nine divisions of the body for this purpose.

Name.	No.	Limb deficient, malformed, injured, or diseased.	Tattoo Marks.					Moles or Warts.	Other Marks.
			Anchor or Cross	Man or Woman	Ship or Flag	Heart or Star	Other Marks		

A "scar on the forehead" was so common a mark of the criminal class, that, unlike the brand of Cain, it had no distinguishing value. One curious point, which has surely escaped the notice of writers of detective stories, was that in Liverpool "special registers are kept of the maiden names of the wives and mothers of criminals, as it is found that in a large proportion of cases an offender, when he changes his name, takes either his wife's or his mother's." It is curious that, in France, a criminal more readily gives his own name correctly than in this country, but the trustworthiness of the finger-print records is now slowly working to a similar frame of mind among English recidivists. Photographs had been taken, as they are now to some extent, and they are, indeed, often most useful. Certain "routes" were arranged, and the forms and photographs were sent round the circuit of police stations, so as to be returned within the usual week of remand. Remarks on these forms were not used as evidence, but were used for official guidance only. The word "photograph" seems now (1912) to comprehend the taking of finger-prints in the official method with ordinary printer's ink.

With all the precautions then available, it was found that mistakes in identification involved unjust suffering. A man named Coyle was sentenced for larceny in 1889, a Millbank warder swearing to his previous conviction, ten years before, as one Hart. The jury having examined Hart's photograph gave a hostile verdict, the distinctive marks of the two men were found to be different, and Coyle moreover showed that he had been doing a short term when Hart was in prison. As is wisely stated in p. 23 of the Report: "The true test of the efficiency of a system of identification is not the number of identifications made, but the number of mis-identifications, or of failure to identify."

A woman lacking her left breast was identified with another who had suffered in the same way, and who had been previously convicted. It became clear that the women were different, and poor Eliza —— had her punishment accordingly reduced from seven years' penal servitude to six months' imprisonment.

A case in 1908 was that of two men charged with burglary, both of whom were short of a fore-finger, and were about the same age and of similar appearance.

A man named Blake was found under circumstances that suggested an attempt at burglary, and was identified by a constable and several others, including a prison warder, as a convict called Steed, under supervision. It was found, however, that Blake had clearly been at liberty when Steed was in prison, and the former was promptly acquitted.

One Callan was convicted as an incorrigible rogue, but had been identified wrongly with another man, he himself at the time of the alleged offence certainly having been in St. George's Workhouse. He was, however, afterwards rightly convicted for a similar offence. It would appear from these and numerous other cases not referred to in this Report, that those mistakes affect only the criminal class. Probably there is a little too much readiness to identify a known rogue with the offender wanted, and those unfortunate victims often of disease and early training deserve fair and just dealing. Alas, however, the really innocent have sometimes suffered dreadfully from judicial blunders. The famous Beck case is too recent and tragic to require recall.

But, besides occasional false identifications of innocent persons, the old system, now happily superseded, was admittedly very ineffective in detecting old offenders passing under different disguises and with false names. The time spent on each identification of old offenders was very great, an average of eight hours being required for one identification. A few minutes is now found to be sufficient.

Tattoo marks are not always so small or so restricted in character as they are found to be by the English police. In *Knowledge* of April, 1911, I had printed in colours a wonderful reproduction of a painting made for me in Japan, of a servant of mine, whose body was finely tattooed over its whole surface, barring face, hands, and feet, in different colours. It had cost him many years' suffering and a small fortune in money to achieve, but he was rather proud of it. I have seen many such examples, though few so fine as a work of art. Extensive tattooing is also common among Italian criminals, the whole body being adorned.

Simple tattoo marks cannot be entirely effaced, but may be defaced; a simple design being made more complicated or altered so as to mislead entirely. A Leeds warder said in evidence before Mr. Asquith's Committee, that : "Tattoo marks are sometimes defaced. I know one case where a person had a letter D on left breast; it is now made into 'Mermaid.' This is sometimes done to prevent recognition in prison. Sometimes the tattoo is removed, but a flesh mark of same shape left."

Our Home Office was indisposed to move hastily in such a matter as finger-print evidence of identity suggested by Englishmen. Another system, very excellent in its way, had the immense advantage of being of foreign origin. As the result, however, of several years' experience, some inherent defects in Mons. Bertillon's anthropometric system—adopted in a modified form by our authorities in 1894—were brought into notice. It was found to be rather delicate for everyday practice, and the fine measurements taken officially often varied. In 1901 therefore, a fresh Committee, with Lord Belper as chairman, was appointed, but no report seems ever to have been published. Soon afterwards, in July, 1902, the Home Secretary directed the introduction of a system of identification based upon finger-prints only, in supersession of the French method of identifying by bodily measurements in a certain order. The results soon showed that the tardy decision had been immediately justified. There was greater certainty assured of valid identifications, the labour was much less, the expense was diminished, and a great danger of false identification was effectively removed.

That the system had taken root was soon evidenced by many newspaper paragraphs of subsequent date. Here is a bit of every-day evidence from a criminal case which resulted in conviction. It appeared in the columns of the *Daily Chronicle*, as far back as December 2nd, 1903. Many such cases were never reported at all. The witness, we are told, had "not the slightest shadow of a doubt that the finger-prints of Elliott were identical with those in the records of Scotland Yard. He might be considered an expert in the matter of finger-prints. Altogether he had dealt with about 500,000 cases of finger-prints." To this report may be added a sentence from that of *The Times*, of the same date: "He had never known the finger-prints of different persons to agree." The witness is significantly described as Detective-Sergeant Collins, of the Finger-Print Office, Scotland Yard. At a later date the same witness (now Inspector Collins), bearing evidence as to the Houndsditch murders, stated that they had now 170,000 different sets of prints recorded. He added that, "During the last ten years, since the introduction of the system in 1901, they had made upwards of 62,000 identifications and recognitions, and, so far as he knew, without error. They dealt, therefore, with pretty large numbers, and he was justified in saying that he had never found two impressions of different fingers to agree." [*The Daily Mail*, February 25th, 1911.]

In *The Daily Mail* of August 10th, 1910, Inspector Munro, of the Finger-print Department of Scotland Yard, in giving evidence that an imprint on a broken window was that of the accused's right middle finger, added: "There had never been any mistake yet in finger-print identification."

One Cris Keegan, who received five years' penal servitude at Dublin in June, 1910, had left a finger-print on a broken church window at Rathmichael. His counsel, pleading guilty for him, said: [*The Daily Mail*, June 10th, 1910] "That when, before the magistrates the accused supplied the best testimony to the finger-print system which it had yet received, by saying 'The taking of these finger-prints is the greatest invention for the detection of criminals. I throw myself on the mercy of the court. I did visit the church.'" This poor man had been convicted forty times before.

Mr. William Henry, a witness in the case, who was in charge of the register for criminals in Dublin castle, said, "he had put through his hands about 150,000 finger-prints, and no two had ever been found alike. This system of identification had now superseded all other methods, and he regarded it as infallible." Witness, having examined the prisoner's fingers in the dock, then said, "the finger-print on the glass had been made by the prisoner's right fore-finger."

Criminals, dreading this kind of evidence, have of late taken sometimes to destroying their ridge-patterns on the fingers. They sometimes also remove and clean a window-pane which they have touched. In the early part of the fourteenth century, clerks in holy orders claimed what was called "benefit of clergy," that is, the privilege of being tried for certain crimes by ecclesiastical courts only, a privilege which was afterwards extended to all persons who could read—for reading was a somewhat rare accomplishment in those merry old times. In 1487 this benefit was restricted, so that a mere layman who was able to read could secure it only once, and then he was to be *branded on the thumb*, to show that he had already enjoyed his one opportunity, thus carefully obliterating by legal methods the best means of proving the fact.

A Leeds man, charged with burglary, was stated in *The Daily Mail* of April 14th, 1908, to have destroyed every one of his finger-ends so that his prints could not be taken. He had been convicted several times before, and had been sentenced to three months' imprisonment.

The complete burglar's outfit now includes well-fitting gloves as an essential element, quite as important as skeleton keys and regulation jemmies. This fact is curiously applied by the late John Davidson, who says, in *Mammon and His Message*: "The gloves of party, of culture, of creed, wherewith men hide their finger-prints lest they should be caught in the act of being themselves, I decline to wear."

Early in 1904, an office in Bradford was broken into by smashing a glass panel in the door. Some cash and postage stamps were secured by the robber. On one piece of glass a single finger-mark had been imprinted accidentally, which was found by the police to be that of a suspected person whose impressions had been officially secured some time before. The offender was duly charged with the crime and convicted. The photographs in this case were reproduced in *The Strand Magazine* of May, 1905, one being the enlarged impression found on the piece of glass, and the other that of the supposed corresponding impression, which was that of the prisoner's left thumb. Those finger-prints resemble, but their mutual likeness is by no means quite conclusive and convincing. Mr. Mallet, the author of the "Finger-Prints which have Convicted Criminals," however, says: "The reader will see how precisely similar are the impressions, and he will be interested, with the aid of a microscope, in seeing how exactly the almost countless ridges and characteristics of the thumb are faithful doubles." The patterns are both enlarged so greatly that not even a lens is required for their discernment, and the "countless ridges" do not run above forty. The two figures are not equalized in their enlargement and comparison is made unnecess-arily difficult, but when made, the curves for some reason cannot be got to agree. The officially registered impression affords clear lineations, but that on the bit of glass panel is muddled and smudgy. On the whole I should not call it a good example of this kind of identification.

A second case given is that of an imprint on a small box which had been used for containing homœopathic remedies. Some cash had been stolen on a certain Saturday night, and on Friday the delinquent was captured and convicted by means of his finger-prints.

The reproduced photographs show the pattern to be somewhat simple, and, allowing for a certain inevitable faintness due to indirect reproduction, the evidence is good of its kind. A pattern of somewhat greater complexity would have afforded much stronger evidence. The chances of a single finger-print of very simple design, so to say, being repeated in the case of another person, is not to be ignored, and if the suspected smudge is obscure the evidence ceases to be of much value.

Of the third case mentioned, we are assured that "without the finger-print it would have been impossible to convict." Now, the enlarged imprint of the suspect's right middle finger has been printed quite clearly, and has good, unique characteristics, but just where these would be most useful for identification the lines in the suspected smudge are fatally blurred and useless for comparison.

A better case is that of a print on a drinking-glass, which was brought out in the way dealt with in a previous chapter of this work. The pattern was rather striking, and the resemblance convincing. The prisoner afterwards confessed his guilt and assisted the police to arrest another man and to recover some stolen property.

In an old French reading book I learned from in earlier days, there was a story of a country doctor who in visiting an upland farmer's wife could find no paper or ink for his prescription. So he wrote his orders in chalk on the farm door and told them to take that to the chemist. They took the door. It seems that a chief detective of Bradford found a bath-room door imprinted in circumstances that aroused suspicion. Protected carefully by paper the door was conveyed on a cart to the Town Hall, as evidence in the case.

Identification does not merely ensure the conviction of the guilty. A very pleasing example was sent to me by an eminent American author and journalist, which shows how the legal use of finger-print evidence established the innocence of an accused negro. Briefly, the story was this. A murder had been committed in Kansas by a coloured man named William West. While looking for him it turned out that the police had just placed under arrest for some minor offence, a young negro named William West, who, however, stoutly maintained his innocence of the murder. The French method of bodily measurements was applied, and the person under arrest was found to correspond exactly in his dimensions in trunk and limbs with those of the sought-for murderer. It remained now only to take the imprints of his finger-tips, a method not long before introduced in that State. It was then clearly seen that, by their decided divergences in pattern, the man in custody could not be the guilty person, although name, colour, and measurements all agreed in the two men. A few days later the real murderer was arrested. The report sent by my friend concludes thus: "The coincidences of name and figure might have been fatal to the innocent man, if the impression of the finger-tips had not also been employed as a means of identification. The police say that this test is infallible. The impression of one man's finger-tips never corresponds exactly with those of any other man."

The system is now largely used in many of the States. Mr. W. A. Pinkerton, the well-known Sherlock Holmes of America, has a high opinion of the validity of the method, and wrote me on his recent visit to this country that he intended to study the subject more closely.

A curious incident happened many years ago to a doctor in the district where I live. Returning from a visit at a late hour, by a lonely road, he was suddenly assailed by a powerful ruffian who tried to garrot him. The doctor, a notably athletic man, objecting to the treatment, finally got one of his assailant's fingers into his mouth and amputated it neatly with his teeth. Early in the morning the rogue came to the same doctor's surgery unwittingly, seeking for surgical help, was seized, and ultimately convicted, getting heavy punishment. Now, on telling this true story (the finger is still kept in spirit) to Mr.—now Sir Charles E.—Troup, at the Home Office, that gentleman smilingly said such a case would never by any chance occur again. Well, in October, 1909, a constable patrolling St. John's Street, Clerkenwell, found, sticking on a spike at the top of a gate, a bloody finger with a ring on it. This was promptly submitted to the police experts at Scotland Yard, who were convinced that it had belonged to a man known as "William Mitchell." A man called "May," with his hand bleeding and bandaged up had just been arrested. It was then found that he had just lost a finger, which he admitted had been done when he was hurriedly getting over the gate. He got twelve months' hard labour, as consolation.

Many years ago I endeavoured to show the value of this method in the recognition of the dead, where records existed. The importance it might acquire is illustrated by the case of a man killed on the Great Western Railway at Slough. His body had been badly shattered and mutilated, and nothing was found in the poor man's pockets but a match-box and a tobacco pipe. Superintendent Pearman sent the finger-prints of the dead man to Scotland Yard, where it was established beyond any doubt that the deceased was one Walter James Downes, a farrier, of Deal. How he came to be known at Scotland Yard is not stated in the newspaper report. The record of a blameless life would have permitted him to rest in a nameless grave.

In some parts of the Continent means are used systematically to identify, by their finger-prints, all vagrants and tramps. It would seem to be clear that in this country a large proportion of those poor waifs are not really criminals in disposition, being often merely failures from physical or mental incapacity, persons hopelessly inefficient in performing the simplest tasks of an industrial life. Among those there is ever a floating population of professional criminals, and others again who are not chronic evildoers, but have, perhaps, once been guilty of some grave offence which has separated them from home and friends.

The Chief Constable of Halifax, in his annual report (1909) deplores the absence of any means of discriminating between the "honest hard-up" and the habitual tramps, who are often rogues and vagabonds. He advocates a central registry for the United Kingdom, based on the finger-print method. This, he thought, would reduce the number of beggars, and would give the genuine but unfortunate worker indisputable evidence as to the purity of his record, and entitle him to more generous treatment in his search of work.

Amongst other evidences that the English method has come to stay, one might quote the prospectus of the Birmingham University Medical Course (1911). There we are informed that the course of Forensic Medicine (Professor Morrison) now includes "Finger-prints and Foot-marks."

In Stoke-on-Trent, the method of finger-prints is reported to have saved the borough both time and money, as compared with the old photographic method. The Chief Constable reported that in Hanley, in 1908 (now incorporated with Stoke): "The finger impressions of seven prisoners, whose antecedents were unknown, were taken by the police, and forwarded to the Registrar of Habitual Criminals, and in six of the cases the impressions were identified as those of persons previously convicted of crime." As had been done in a previous report, it is also stated, that "a considerable amount is annually saved to the department by the discontinuance of the photographing of prisoners, excepting where special circumstances make it desirable or necessary."

According to the *Evening Post*, the leading financial journal of New York, the new system of finger-prints is rapidly growing in favour with bankers who have been recently victimised by swindlers and forgers. The Williamsburg Savings Bank was the first institution to adopt the system. Other banks, finding it entailed much delay, appointed a special clerk, whose duty it is to persuade ladies to remove their gloves and submit to the inking operation.

A New York lawyer, Mr. F. R. Fast, advocated some years ago a finger-print method of attesting legal documents, as by the old-fashioned seal now disused, except in a few high official cases. His suggestion was that a man should choose one of his ten fingers, the one which happens to have most individuality about it, perhaps, as his "Ego" finger, with which to adhibit his impression after his usual written signature, in law papers, cheques, and the like. He also advocated storing past (in regard to wills, etc.) impressions of all the ten fingers. This has always been my contention, that the ten fingers should be used in cases requiring great security. One or more should also be adhibited in the case of illiterate persons who now sign with a cross. With passports, this is now actually done in several countries on the European continent. It ought at once, I think, to be adopted by bankers, for circular notes—a great convenience to travellers having to use different currencies, but who may sometimes find it difficult to get a friend to identify them. The case of pensioners, old age and others, would seem to be urgent now, and, as a medical man, I cannot help thinking that present official methods are rather loose and may lead to frequent abuses. A general practitioner is asked to sign a certificate of identity in circumstances where it is not easy to be certain. A good-natured, busy doctor may aid roguery by simply echoing what an applicant, or his friends, may have suggested.

In criminal trials, an English jury ought to be afforded some safeguard as to identity. A supposed old convict who had become a constable fell again into evil ways, but was soon found out by a comparison of fresh finger-prints, with records which he had not at first been suspected of having left behind. He had had a good character in the army. The jury in this case very properly insisted on being thoroughly satisfied by their own examination of the finger-print evidence submitted to the court. Not all juries are quite complaisant on this point. I was present at a case in which very pertinent and intelligent questions were asked by one or two sceptical jurymen, and a demonstration of the printing process done before them was insisted upon.

In one Old Bailey case the jury finally rejected evidence of this kind. The comment of a London newspaper was this :—

> "In finger-print cases the police expert is generally trusted implicitly, and the jury is apt to be forgetful of the fact that, although the theory of finger-prints has been reduced almost to an exact science, mistakes may be made in applying it, and the policeman has frequently an over-anxiety to prove his case that may distort his view."

The true cure for this evil, which has often been pointed out, would seem to be the systematic instruction of the police force—or some select numbers of them—in all such matters as come within their official duties. With eight years' experience as a police surgeon, I must say that a great deal of the valuable kind of evidence that recent fiction has made popular is spoiled by the methods of the average constable. Professor Glaister, the eminent medical jurist of Glasgow, was, I think, the first to give a place to finger-print evidence in a work on Forensic Medicine. The second edition of his work is fully illustrated with specimens. We have seen that the study of finger- and foot-prints now forms a regular subject in the medical course of Birmingham University. It would be easy to arrange, at local centres, such instruction in this method as is now frequently given to constables in ambulance work. To some extent this, I believe, has already been done, but the teachers themselves evidently need to be taught some elemental principles to instruct effectively. The huge records left in Scotland Yard and other police centres of administration have not as yet done any service to the biological aspects of Dactylography. They are silent and still as the rocks were before Hutton and Lyell struck them with the rod of science and made living springs gush out in great abundance.

GLOSSARY

OF SOME TERMS USED BY DACTYLOGRAPHERS.

ACCIDENTALS. Nondescript patterns in the class composites.

ANTHROPOID. Of the great man-like apes (gorilla, orang-utan, and chimpanzee).

ANTHROPOMETRIC. Bodily measurements.

ANTHROPOMETRY. Science of accurate bodily measurements.

ARCH. A curved set of lineations, without backward turn; a bow.

BERTILLONAGE. Alphonse Bertillon's anthropometric methods.

BIFURCATION. Fork-like splitting into two branches.

BLUR. A dull, smudgy imprint.

BOW. A curved lineation like a bow.

BULB. The pad of a finger-tip.

CHARACTERISTIC. Any striking feature in a pattern which gives distinctiveness.

CHIRALITY. The principle involved in "Mirror Patterns."

COMPOSITE. Patterns composed of various elements, such as arch, loop, or whorl.

CORE. The heart or central portion of a finger-print.

CREASE (*palmar*). The lines which indicate folding of the hand surface.

DACTYLOGRAPH. A finger-impression taken by any process.

DACTYLOLITE. An indented finger-print as on wax.

DACTYLOSCOPY (*Daktyloskopie*). The practical study of Finger-prints.

DELTA. A somewhat triangular figure formed by skin lineations.

DERMA, DERMAL. The deep true skin, the "quick."

DIGIT, DIGITAL. A finger, of fingers.

EPIDERMIS. The upper skin which readily peels off.

EPITHELIUM. The scaly surface of skin.

EXHIBIT. An article to be shown in court as evidence.

"FLEXIBLE CURVES." An instrument for measuring enlarged curving lineations.

FORK. A Y-like figure.

FORMULA (pl. FORMULÆ). The arrangement of syllables or signs to denote a set of finger-prints.

FURROW. The hollow line between ridges, a *sulcus*.

HOOK. A J-like figure in any position.

INDEX FINGER. The finger used in pointing.

JUNCTION. Where two lineations meet or break off.

LINEATION. A line as printed, whether ridge or furrow.

LOOP. A curved line which returns on itself.

MICROMETER. An instrument like a pair of compasses, used for fine measurements.

MIRROR PATTERN. The reverse (exact) image of a given figure.

NEGATIVE. A print in which the ridges are white and furrows black, as when smoked glass is used.

PALMAR. Of front surface of the hand.

PAPILLA (pl. PAPILLÆ). Elements in a ridge where touch organs are.

"PHOTOGRAPH." Used sometimes legally for finger-prints.

POCKET LOOP. A variety of imperfect loop.

POSITIVE. A finger-print where ridges appear black (or other colour of pigment used) and furrows are white.

PRIMATES. An order of animals, including lemurs, monkeys, apes, and man.

RADIAL. The thumb side of the hand (opposed to *Ulnar.*)

RECOGNITION. An identification.

RECIDIVIST. A relapsing or incorrigible criminal.

RIDGE. A line of skin tissue, elevated, with sweat-pores.

ROD. A figure like a rod.

ROLLED PRINT. A finger-print not taken by direct or plain impress, but by a revolution of the inked surface on flat paper.

RUGA (pl. RUGÆ). A ridge.

SEARCHER. One who seeks for a former registration.

SEBACEOUS. Of the greasy excretion of the skin.

SMUDGE. A blurred or dull imprint.

STAPLE. A figure like a U inverted ; thus, ∩.

SUDOR. Sweat.

SUDORIPAROUS. Of sweat, sweat-yielding.

SULCUS (pl. SULCI). A skin groove or furrow.

TWINNED LOOP. Two adjoining loops in a core, complementary in position.

TENTED ARCH. An arch shaped like a tent or volcanic mountain.

TERMINUS. A term used for distinctive points within and without a core.

ULNAR. The little finger side of the hand. (Opposed to *Radial*).

VERSO. May be used for an imprint as the converse of the fleshy pattern.

WHORL. A flat spiral figure.

WIDDERSHINS. The reverse of a clock-hand's movement.

SHORT BIBLIOGRAPHY.

ASQUITH'S COMMITTEE.—[Blue Book.] "Identification of Habitual Criminals," 1894.

CLEMENS, S. L. (Mark Twain.).—"Pudd'nhead Wilson" A story illustrating the principles of Finger-Print Identification.

DARWIN, CHARLES.—"Origin of Species," 1859; "Descent of Man," 1871.

DEVON, JAMES.—"The Criminal and the Community," 1912.

"ENCYCLOPÆDIA BRITANNICA."—"Finger Prints," etc., 1911.

FAULDS, HENRY.—"On the Skin-furrows of the hands," (*Nature*, chap. xxii., p. 605), 1880; "Dactyloscopy" (St. Thomas's Hospital *Gazette*), January, 1904; "Guide to Finger-Print Identification," 1905; "Finger Prints: a chapter in the History of their use for Personal Identification," (*Knowledge*), April, 1911.

FERRERO, G. L.—"Criminal Man" (Lombroso's), 1911.

FORGEOT, RENE.—"Les empreintes latentes" (Thesis), 1891.

GALTON, FRANCIS.—"Identification by Finger-Tips" (*The Nineteenth Century*), August, 1891; "Finger Prints, 1892; "Finger-Print Directories, 1895.

GARSON, J. G.—"Finger-Prints Classification" (*Jour. Anthrop. Inst.*, chap. xxx. p. 101), 1900.

GLAISTER, J.—"Textbook of Medical Jurisprudence," 1902 (and 2nd edition).

GRAY, H.—" Anatomy, Descriptive and Surgical" (16th ed.) 1905.

HADDON, A. C.—"Races of Man, and their Distribution," 1909; "History of Anthropology" 1910.

HENRY, E. R.—"Classification and Uses of Finger-Prints," 1905.

HEPBURN, D.—"The Papillary ridges on monkeys' hands and feet" (*Nature*, vol. liii., 36), 1895.

HERSCHEL, W. J.—"Skin Furrows of the Hand," *Nature*, vol. xxii., 76), 1880.

HOPF, LUDWIG. "The Human Species" (Eng. trans.) 1909.

LINDSAY, B.—" Animal Life."

MARETT, R.—" Anthropology."

MITCHELL. "Science and the Crimiral," 1911.

PURKINJE, J. E. "Commentatio de examine physiologico organi visus et systematis cutanei," 1823.

SCHLAGINHAUFEN, OTTO. "Der Hautleistensystem der Primatenplanta" (with a valuable bibliography), *Gegenbaur's Jahrbuch*, 1905.

SCHOFIELD, A. T. "Elementary Physiology for Students," 1892.

STEWART, G. N. "Manual of Physiology," 1910.

THOMSON, J. A., and P. GEDDES. "Evolution," 1911.

TYLOR. "Primitive Culture," 1903.

WALKER, N. "Introduction to Dermatology," 1904.

WALLACE, A. R. "The World of Life," 1910.

WINDT and KODICEK. "Daktyloskopie," 1904.

INDEX.

MILNER AND CO., PRINTERS, HALIFAX.

THE ORIGIN OF FINGER-PRINTING

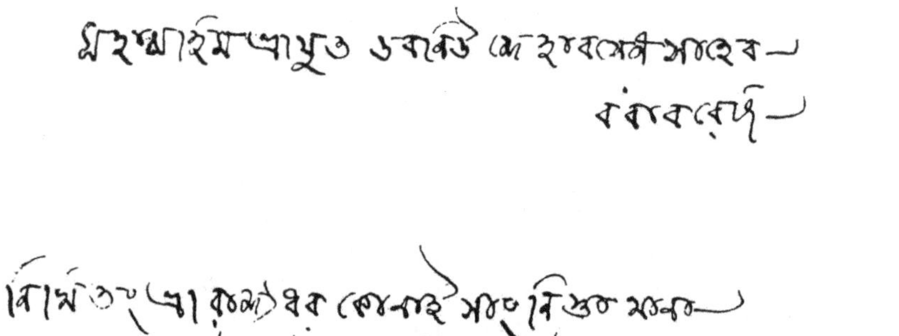

Contract for 2,000 maunds of road-metalling, between W. J. Herschel and Rajyadhar Konai, in Konai's handwriting.

See page 8.

THE ORIGIN OF FINGER-PRINTING

BY

SIR WILLIAM J. HERSCHEL, BART.

HUMPHREY MILFORD
OXFORD UNIVERSITY PRESS
LONDON EDINBURGH GLASGOW
NEW YORK TORONTO MELBOURNE BOMBAY
1916

PRINTED IN ENGLAND
AT THE OXFORD UNIVERSITY PRESS

DEDICATION

TO SIR EDWARD HENRY, G.C.V.O., K.C.B., C.S.I.

Commissioner of the Metropolitan Police.

I am offering you this old story of the beginnings of Finger-printing, by way of expressing my warm and continuous admiration of those masterly developments of its original applications, whereby, first in Bengal and the Transvaal, and then in England, you have fashioned a weapon of penetrating certainty for the sterner needs of Justice.

W. J. HERSCHEL.

June, 1916.

PREFACE

THE following pages have two objects: first, to place on record the genesis of the Finger-print method of personal identification, from its discovery in Bengal in 1858, till its public demonstration there in 1877–8; secondly, to examine the scanty suggestions of evidence that this use of our fingers had been foreshadowed in Europe more than a hundred years ago, and had indeed been general in ancient times, especially in China.

In later years, and in energetic hands, the method has been developed into a system far more effective than anything I contemplated, and I do not go into that part of the story; but I believe these pages will suffice to show the originality of my study of its two essential features, the strict individuality and the stubborn persistence of the patterns on our fingers.

The gift granted to me of lighting upon a discovery which promised escape from one great difficulty of administration in India is more than ever appreciated by me since I have lived to see the promise wonderfully fulfilled there, and in other lands as well.

For the sake of interest I give, among the illustrations, several examples of late 'repeats' taken many years after I left India; but these do not belong to my story.

LIST OF ILLUSTRATIONS

THE ORIGIN OF FINGER-PRINTING

In 1858, after five years' service, as an Assistant under the old East India Company, in the interior of Bengal, I was in charge of my first subdivision, the head-quarters of which were then at Jungipoor, on the upper reaches of the Hooghly river. My executive and magisterial experience had by that time forced on me that distrust of all evidence tendered in Court which did so much to cloud our faith in the people around us. We cannot be too thankful that things have greatly improved in India in the last sixty years, but the time of which I am speaking was the very worst time of my life in this respect. I remember only too well writing in great despondency to one of the best and soberest-minded of my senior companions at Haileybury[1] about my despair of any good coming from orders and decisions based on such slippery facts, and the comfort I found in his sensible reply.

It happened, in July of that year, that I was starting the first bit of road metalling at Jungipoor, and invited tenders for a supply of 'ghooting' (a good binding material for light roads). A native named Rājyadhar Kōnāi, of the village of Nistā, came to terms with me, and at my desire drew up our agreement in his own hand, in true commercial style. He was about to sign it in the usual way, at the upper right-hand

[1] Till 1857 the East India Company's College.

corner, when I stopped him in order to read it myself; and it then occurred to me to try an experiment by taking the stamp of his hand, by way of signature instead of writing. There was nothing very original about that, as an idea. Many must have heard of some such use of a man's hand; and the correspondence that has taken place has brought to light old instances of the hand, or the nail of a finger, or the teeth in one's mouth, being used to certify a man's act, or a woman's. But these have all been isolated instances. Sir Francis Galton, however, has pointed out[1] that in our own times the engraver Bewick had a fancy for engraving his thumb-mark, with his name attached, as vignettes, or as colophons, in books which he published.[2] As a boy I had loved Bewick on Birds: I regret that it is not now to be found in our library. Galton's remark has reminded me that I used to see the thumb-mark there, as well as I recollect, in an ornamental title-page. I mention this because I dare say it had something to do with my fascination over Kōnāi's hand-markings. If so, the influence was unknown to me. The absorbing interests of manhood had blotted out, not Bewick, but his thumb-mark, from my memory. However that may be, I was only wishing to frighten Kōnāi out of all thought of repudiating his signature hereafter. He, of course, had never dreamt of such an attestation, but fell in readily enough. I dabbed his palm and fingers over with the home-made oil-ink used

[1] 'Finger-prints' (Macmillan, 1892), p. 26. [2] See Appendix.

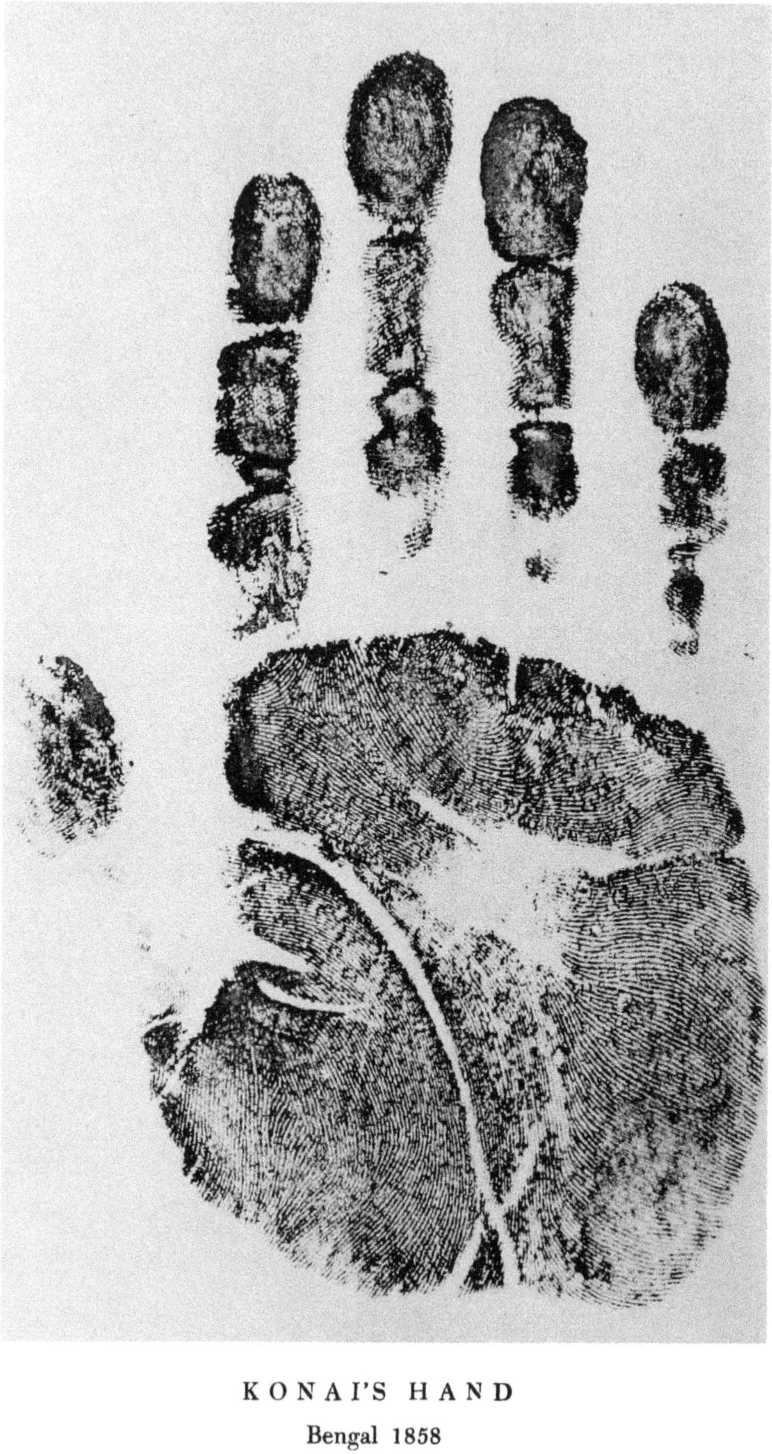

KONAI'S HAND

Bengal 1858

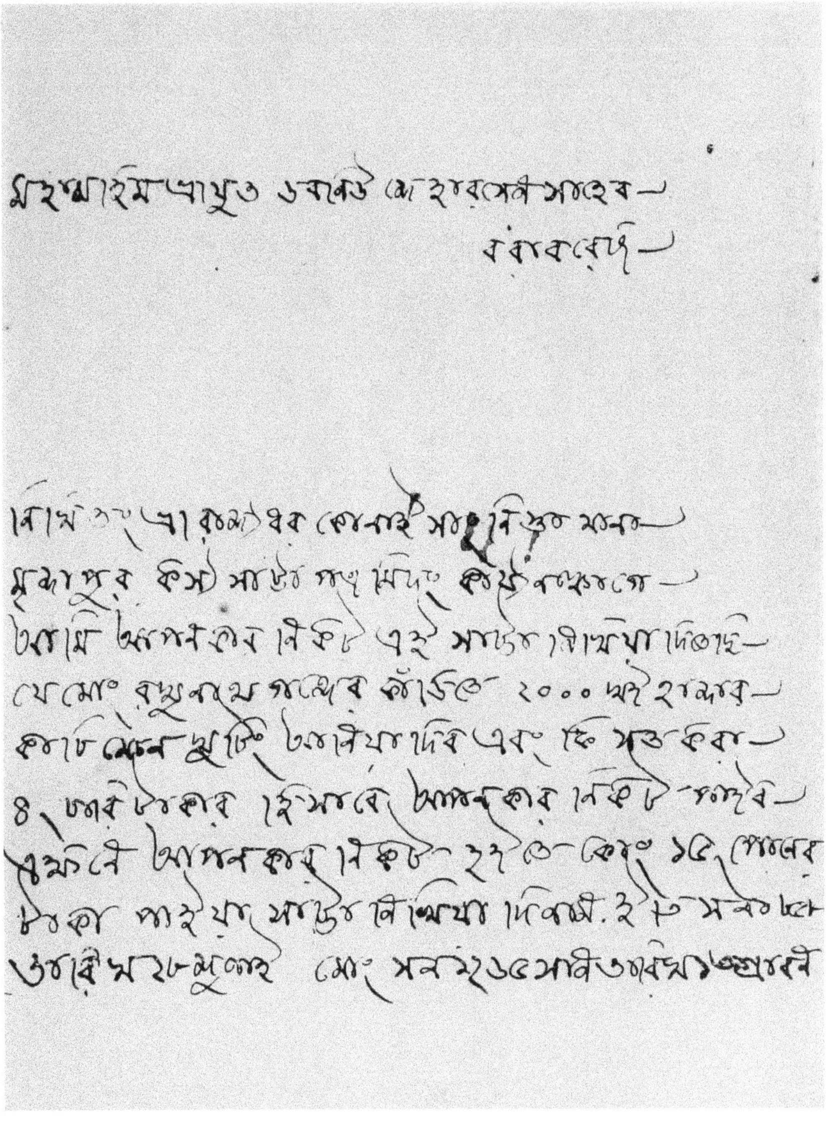

Contract for 2,000 maunds of road-metalling, between W. J. Herschel and Rajyadhar Konai, in Konai's handwriting

for my official seal and pressed the whole hand on the back of the contract, and we studied it together, with a good deal of chaff about palmistry, comparing his palm with mine on another impression. Here is a facsimile of the whole document, made by the Clarendon Press. I was so pleased with the experiment that, having to make a second contract with Kōnāi, I made him attest it in the same way. One of these contracts I gave to Sir Francis (then Mr.) Galton for his celebrated paper read before the Royal Society, November 1890, to which body he presented it; the other lies before me now. Trials with my own fingers soon showed the advantage of using them instead of the whole hand for the purpose then in view, i.e. for securing a signature which the writer would obviously hesitate to disown. That he might be infallibly convicted of perjury, if he did, is a very different matter. That was not settled, and could not have been settled, to the satisfaction of Courts of Justice, till, after many years, abundant agreement had been reached among ordinary people. The very possibility of such a sanction' (to use a technical expression) to the use of a finger-print did not dawn upon me till after long experience, and even then it became no more than a personal conviction for many years more. The decisiveness of a finger-print is now one of the most powerful aids to Justice. Our possession of it derives from the impression of Kōnāi's hand in 1858.

Of trials with my own fingers the oldest impression I possess was taken in June 1859, when I first began to keep records. I had been transferred to be Magistrate of Arrah, the most north-westerly district of Bengal, where the Mutiny still left work to do which allowed little time for private hobbies; but I took so many prints among the society of the Station, as well as among Indians of all classes, that my 'fad' about them was well known. The Medical Officer of Arrah was Dr. R. F. Hutchinson, who

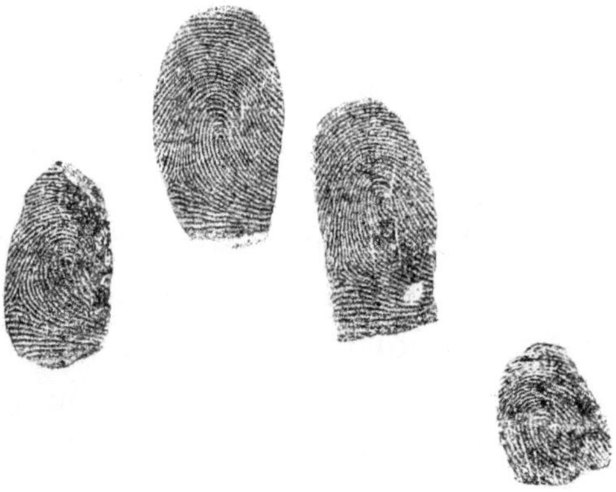

R. F. Hutchinson, June 1859, Medical Officer at Arrah Station.

naturally took great interest in the subject. Twenty-one years later, in 1880, he was still there, and sent me a 'repeat' print of his fingers. Here is a facsimile of his first Arrah impression. In 1890, being in England, he visited Galton's Laboratory, and gave a second repeat (after thirty-one years) which was used in 'Finger-prints' (1892), p. 93, to support Mr. Galton's evidence of 'Persistency'. In the facsimile 'Collection 1858–1913', which I am attaching to some of the copies of this narrative, will be found other prints which I took at Arrah of my whole hand and of my right foot. They agree irresistibly with prints taken now after an interval of fifty-seven years.

In 1860 I was sent as Magistrate to Nuddea, nearer to Calcutta. The Indigo disturbances in the district had given rise to a great deal of violence, litigation, and fraud; forgery and perjury were rampant. The rent-rolls of the ryots put into Court by the Zemindars; the pottahs (agreements for rent) purporting to be issued by them to each ryot, put in by the latter; the kabooliyats (acceptances) purporting to be signed by the ryot, and tendered in evidence against him; all these documents were frequently worth no more than the paper on which they were written. In my own jail a notorious convict was found making clay seals of well-known landlords, and forging their signatures on pottahs smuggled into his hands. He was detected by the colour of the floor of his cell, where he kept his stock-in-trade buried. Things were so bad in this and other ways that the administration of Civil Justice had unusual difficulty in preserving its dignity. I was driven to take up finger-prints now with a definite object before me, and for three years continued taking a very large number from all sorts and conditions of men. I give here some selected impressions of friends taken in Nuddea during the years 1860, 1861, and 1862, in order of date, and names of some others.

1860, July. Claude Brown, a prominent merchant of Calcutta, who was making a tour in the Indigo districts, and was at the time my guest.

1860, July 29. Captain H. Raban, Head of the Bengal Police, sent to Nuddea on account of its disturbed state; also my guest. He took extreme interest in the evidence of his own imprint. It was my habit, of course, to give duplicates of his 'mark' to every one of importance.

r. 1 r. 2

Captain H. Raban, Head of the Police in Lower Bengal, July 29, 1860.

1860, July 31. W. Waterfield, B.C.S., a college friend, afterwards Comptroller-General of the Treasuries of India. I have several 'repeats' of his; see especially p. 29.

1861, June 24. Ogilvie Temple, Judge of the Court of Small Causes, Kooshtea.

1862, April 13. At a gathering at my house at Kishnagar I had the good fortune to secure the prints of many other notables of the district.

The Mahārājā of Nuddea. He was the highest of the old nobility of Bengal. He was much struck, as I was, by the remarkable symmetry of the 'pattern' on one of his fingers at the core.

r. 1 r. 2
April 13, 1862.
Mahārājā of Nuddea.

Enlarged for the remarkable pattern of r. 1.

Same day. E. Grey, B.C.S. A college friend, on my staff, afterwards Civil and Sessions Judge. He, I am happy to say, is still alive (1916), and his 'repeat' is quite good now.

r. 1 r. 2
April 13, 1862.
A. C. Howard.

r. 1 r. 2
July 20, 1908.
Sir Charles Howard.

Same day. A. C. Howard, District Superintendent of Police, Nuddea, afterwards Assistant Commissioner at Scotland Yard, and knighted for his services there, as Sir Charles Howard. He gladly gave me a 'repeat' in London after forty-six years. It will be seen how good the persistence has been.

Same day. Three other Assistant Magistrates on the unusually large staff of the district. Among these was F. K. Hewitt, B.C.S., afterwards Commissioner of Chota Nagpur. Twenty-six years later, at my request, he furnished Sir Francis Galton with the 'repeat' printed on p. 93 of his famous work 'Finger-prints' (Macmillan, 1892). I have much later repeats taken at Oxford.

Same day. Ninian H. Thomson, Judge of the Court of Small Causes. He kindly sent me a repeat twenty-eight years later from Florence, and this also appears in the same work, p. 93.

Very early in my experiments I entertained misgivings about the possibility of the impressions being forged by the professional criminals whom we had so much reason to fear. I therefore submitted some specimens to the best artists in Calcutta to imitate. Their failure sufficed to dispel all anxiety on that point. None of them come near Bewick's engravings in accuracy.

Before I left Kishnagar (Nuddea) the violence of the Indigo disturbances had been subdued, but the Courts became choked with suits for enhancement of rent upon the recalcitrant cultivators, and the sore point about the genuineness of leases, &c., became aggravated. I took courage from despair, and in my judicial capacity (if I remember right) addressed an official letter to the Government of Bengal, definitely advocating administrative action to enforce the use of 'finger-prints' by both parties as necessary to the validity of these documents.

Unfortunately I kept no private draft of this letter, and have lost the date, probably 1862 or 1863. It must, however, be on record, both in Nuddea and in the Calcutta Secretariat. Nothing came of it, and I took no more pains about it. But a few years ago I was pleasantly reminded by Mr. Horace Cockerell, for some time Secretary to the Government, who gave me the history of its reception, viz. that it had been deemed inadvisable, when things were quieting down, to raise a new controversy of the sort. He added that it was a matter of regret now, that no action whatever had been taken, but he pointed out that legislation would have been necessary to make the new marks admissible in evidence, and to get such a law on the spur of the moment would have been hopeless. That difficulty had certainly never occurred to me when I made the suggestion. But how weighty an objection it was is shown by the fact that it was long, even after the value of finger-prints had been established in practice, before the High Court of Calcutta, in a leading case, declared that the evidence could not be excluded, nay more, that it was cogent. This was many years before such a case in England. At the time I wrote it is quite certain that no Court in India, no pleader, no solicitor had ever recognized such signatures as these.

In 1863 I took my first furlough to England, which changed the current of my thoughts. But I found that my own people had been more interested than I had supposed by my correspondence on the subject. Among my brother Alexander's papers was found after his death a letter telling him my ideas, and asking him to devise a roller of some sort, for oil-ink, better than my soft office pads.

During that and later furloughs I took no public steps about the subject. In society, of course, it was looked on simply as a hobby, attracting no more serious attention than did Bewick's fancy for engraving his thumb-mark in his day. But the warm interest shown by my own people, who had known my early troubles in India, determined me, during my last furlough, that before completing my service I would give the thing an open official trial on my own responsibility. I sailed, 1877, in the P. and O. steamer 'Mongolia', Captain Coleman, with my sister, now Mrs. Maclear, who was an enthusiast on my side. We roused attention enough on board in the Indian Ocean to obtain the finger-prints of the Captain and many of his officers, stewards, and kalāshis; also of many of the passengers, among whom I may especially mention Sir Alfred and Lady Lyall (as they afterwards became), Colonel Garrow Waterfield, and Colonel Chermside. Some thirty years later, 1908, Sir A. Lyall permitted me to take and use his repeat impression. Here are facsimiles of both, and also of Captain Coleman's, the pattern of which was thought then to deserve enlargement. Friendship, which for family reasons sprang up between Colonel Garrow Waterfield and myself, led him to take special interest in my project, and I cannot doubt that he carried that with him to the Punjab, where his reputation was high. Most of the other saloon passengers were business men on their way back to the Far East, and left us at Ceylon.

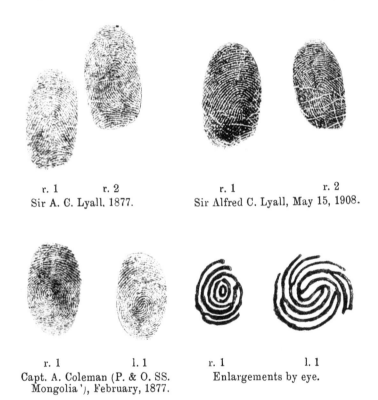

r. 1 r. 2
Sir A. C. Lyall, 1877.

r. 1 r. 2
Sir Alfred C. Lyall, May 15, 1908.

r. 1 l. 1
Capt. A. Coleman (P. & O. SS. Mongolia'), February, 1877.

r. 1 l. 1
Enlargements by eye.

If any one of them had heard of the use of these marks, say in China, I could not but have been told of it. But there was not a breath of the sort. I give here a list of the remaining signatures still in my possession, in case any may meet with recognition: F. Slight, Officer of the 'Mongolia, F. A. Owen, J. Watson, R. Hawkins, F. Wingrove, O. Westphal, J. W. Malet, G. S. Lynch, Mrs. Philip. It is only reasonable, I think, to believe that such a novel and evidently useful idea would have spread by their means wherever they went. My exhibition was frequently asked for, and I always gave a duplicate of his mark to each person, and sometimes added one of my own to show the extraordinary persistence of patterns after nigh twenty years.

On my return to India my position as Magistrate and Collector at Hooghly, near Calcutta, gave me the control, not only of criminal courts, but of the jail, and of the modern Department for Registration of Deeds of all sorts, and among minor duties the payment of Government pensions. Registration, of course, appealed most strongly to my desires, but the Sub-Registrar and his clerks had to be trained, and meanwhile the few pensioners enabled me to break the ice myself. I was not a little anxious lest, officially introduced, Hindus might take alarm for their caste. The memory of the greased cartridges of the Mutiny, so near Hooghly, was indelible. In private experiments I had never met any such difficulty, but the old lesson had been a severe one, and I thought it well, when acting officially, to take every precaution. I was careful, therefore, from the first ostentatiously to employ Hindus to take the impressions wanted; using, as if a matter of course, the pad and the ink made by one of themselves from the very seed-oil and lamp-black which were in constant use for the office seals in the several departments.

The glad approval of the pensioners was a great pleasure to me, and made the other registration work astonishingly easy. The clerks took to it unhesitatingly, and enjoyed the fun of explaining the 'Sahib's hikmat'. No one ever hesitated to do as he was told, or to take away duplicates for talk at home. The process of registration at that time was regulated by a late law devised to afford the best security then possible for the genuineness of deeds, as far as attestation went. The signatures, whether in full or by caste mark, or by cross, or, in the case of women mostly, by touching the paper with the tip of the finger wetted with ink from the clerk's pen (see p. 35), were always made in the presence and under the eye of the Registrar, who, in most cases, had to rely on the sworn evidence of witnesses attesting their personal knowledge of the executant. The Registrar was, of course, responsible for using his intelligence in each case to prevent imposture. His part of the work was never impeached, that I know, in Bengal; nevertheless, fraudulent attempts did still come to light. Signatures were still denied; personations in presenting false deeds did take place, either to swindle, or, in one case, to fabricate an alibi. As long as I was at Hooghly I was quite satisfied that no will or other deed registered there with the new safeguard would ever be repudiated by the actual executant. I have had to think otherwise since then, because many years afterwards a man (in another district) who had given his finger-print before a Registrar repudiated it. He was summoned to give his evidence on oath. It was found that he had cut off the joints of his fingers, hoping to defeat justice by corrupting the witnesses so as to prove that he was *not* the man they had recognized before the Registrar. The High Court rejected the sworn story of an accident, and confirmed the facts of the registration, with the necessary consequence to the offender for his perjury. I do not know of any other repudiation having been pressed to this bitter end in India or elsewhere. The contrast between the inherent weakness of the old law and the efficiency of the new test could not be better exemplified. This case gave the first stern blow to the foul mischief that had developed such cruel proportions in India under cover of our conservative legal habits.

The way the new safeguard was applied at Hooghly in 1877 was thus:—After the legal formalities of registration had been observed, the Registrar made the person print his two fingers on the deed, and again in a diary book which was kept by him in the office, for my own inspection rather than as evidence. It is, no doubt, preserved at Hooghly still.

It was from this book that cuttings were made at my request in 1892 by Mr. Duke, the magistrate, which formed the subject of Sir Francis Galton's volume on 'Blurred Finger-prints' (1893), to which, for its cogency in marshalling the evidence, I must refer my readers. I annex a tracing of one of his enlargements, by permission of the London University, to which he left his great collection.

Another form in which I made use of the new system for public purposes was in the jail. The common device of hiring a substitute to serve out a term was not unknown, but it involved a long risk of detection. A safer but very costly, and

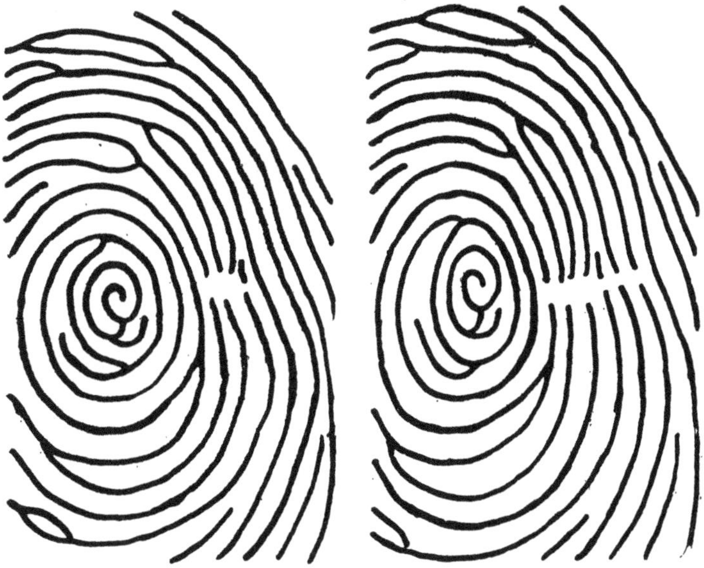

a *b*

Bechā Rām Dās Adhikāri. From tracings by Mr. Galton of enlargements. (*a*) Made in 1877 when registering his deed; (*b*) made in 1892 for Mr. Galton.

therefore rare, device was sham death and a purchased corpse, affording comparative safety after escape. A case of this kind, carried out with the aid of an irregularly appointed doctor, was strongly suspected by me at Hooghly.[1] The precaution I

[1] I had him dismissed soon after for a different offence.

adopted was to take the finger-prints of each offender when passing sentence of imprisonment, both on the records of the Court and also on the warrant to the jailer.

All these processes were in full use when I left India, on the completion of twenty-five years' service, in 1878. I was by that time almost broken down in health, and more so in energy. Sir Ashley Eden, the Lieutenant-Governor, offered me a substantive Commissionership. I had already held such an appointment twice, and nothing but an honest sense of inability made me decline it now. I mention this in explanation of the slackness on my part, but for which the finger-print system would certainly have been put in force in the Registration Department, at least throughout Bengal, forty years ago. As it was, I only tried to induce the Inspector of Jails and the Registrar-General of the day to give the system a trial. Fortunately I kept an office copy of this letter, which, in reply to outside criticism, I published in 'Nature', Nov. 22, 1894, and repeat here to complete this narrative.

(True Copy of Office Copy.)

Hooghly, *August* 15, 1877.

My dear B——,—I enclose a paper which looks unusual, but which I hope has some value. It exhibits a method of identification of persons, which, with ordinary care in execution, and with judicial care in the scrutiny, is, I can now say, for all practical purposes far more infallible than photography. It consists in taking a seal-like impression, in common seal ink, of the markings on the skin of the two forefingers of the right hand (these two being taken for convenience only).

I am able to say that these marks do not (bar accidents) change in the course of ten or fifteen years so much as to affect the utility of the test.

The process of taking the impression is hardly more difficult than that of making a fair stamp of an office seal. I have been trying it in the Jail and in the Registering Office and among pensioners here for some months past. I have purposely taken no particular pains in explaining the process, beyond once showing how it is done, and once or twice visiting the office, inspecting the signatures,[1] and asking the *omlah*[2] to be a little more careful. The articles necessary are such as the *daftari*[3] can prepare on a mere verbal explanation.

Every person who now registers a document at Hooghly has to sign his 'sign-manual'. None has offered the smallest objection, and I believe that the practice, if generally adopted, will put an end to all attempts at personation.

The cogency of the evidence is admitted by every one who takes the trouble to compare a few signatures together, and to try making a few himself. I have taken thousands now in the course of the last twenty years, and (bar smudges and accidents, which are rarely bad enough to be fatal) I am prepared to answer for the identity of every person whose 'sign-manual' I can now produce if I am confronted with him.

As an instance of the value of the thing, I might suggest that if Roger Tichborne had given his 'sign-manual' on entering the Army on any register, the whole Orton case would have been knocked on the head in ten minutes by requiring Orton to make his sign-manual alongside it for comparison.

I send this specimen to you because I believe that identification is by no means the unnecessary thing in jails which one

[1] The words 'signature', 'sign-manual', 'seal', were used indifferently in this letter for 'finger-print'.

[2] Clerks.

[3] Man in charge of stationery.

might presume it should be. I don't think I need dilate on that point. Here is the means of verifying the identity of every man in jail with the man sentenced by the court, at any moment, day or night. Call the number up and make him sign. If it is he, it is he; if not, he is exposed on the spot. Is No. 1302 really dead, and is that his corpse or a sham one? The corpse has two fingers that will answer the question at once. Is this man brought into jail the real Simon Pure sentenced by the magistrate? The sign-manual on the back of the magistrate's warrant is there to testify, &c.

For uses in other departments and transactions, especially among illiterate people, it is available with such ease that I quite think its general use would be a substantial contribution towards public morality. Now that it is pretty well known here, I do not believe the man lives who would dare to attempt personation before the Registrar here. The *mukhtears*[1] all know the potency of the evidence too well.

Will you kindly give the matter a little patient attention, and then let me ask whether you would let me try it in other jails?

The impressions will, I doubt not, explain themselves to you without more words. I will say that perhaps in a small proportion of the cases that might come to question the study of the seals by an expert might be advisable, but that in most cases any man of judgement giving his attention to it cannot fail to pronounce right. I have never seen any two signatures about which I remained in doubt after sufficient care.

Kindly keep the specimens carefully.

Yours sincerely,

W. HERSCHEL.

I received one answer, but its tenor was not so encouraging as I had hoped. I was out of heart, and did not press my request.

How much all this was regretted afterwards by

[1] Solicitors.

others I must in simple justice record. It came about so quietly and so honourably that it is only now that I feel myself free to say publicly how deeply I was touched. My first substantive Commissionership had been given me by Sir George Campbell, to whose house I was not long after brought back in a dying condition from malarial fever. Sir George and his private secretary, Mr. Luttman Johnson, took us, my wife and myself, into the tenderest care. Years afterwards, in 1906, the latter befriended me in the kindliest manner at the annual I. C. S. garden-party, which I but rarely attended, and invited me to dine with him that evening. It was a party of seven or eight, and the next to arrive were Sir James and Lady Bourdillon. His name, when our host introduced us, I only recognized as lately Acting Lieutenant-Governor of Bengal. To my great surprise, before our hands parted, he told me how often he had wished to meet me, to express his constant regret at having let my suggestion slip through his hands when he was Registrar-General. He remembered my letter well, and had indeed taken action by inquiry concerning my doings in his department, but for some reason he had lost sight of the matter. Needless to say, we became the firmest of friends on the spot, and I had the pleasure of a visit from him afterwards at Oxford. It is some years now since he and Mr. Luttman Johnson died. None of us, as far as I know, has ever spoken of this fine act of Sir James's except in strict privacy.

The Inspector of Jails of 1877, Mr. Beverley,

afterwards a judge in the High Court of Bengal, is still alive. Writing in 1906, he says, regretfully, 'I have no recollection of writing the letter you refer to, but I know that, both as Registrar-General and as Inspector of Jails, I took great interest in the Finger-print system of identification, of which I always regarded you as the Apostle in India'. He too came to see me at Oxford after that, with one of his successors in the High Court.

I shall say more farther on in regard to my statement in this 1877 letter that 'these marks do not change in the course of ten or fifteen years'.

During my stay at Hooghly, so near Calcutta, I saw more society in my own house than in other stations, and interested my friends with the novelty of finger-printing. I give a few of their names to which special interest attaches.

Among Indian gentlemen, whose prints were taken at Hooghly in 1877, I do not know who are still living; I can only give the names of

(1) Bābu Dinonāth Pāl, of Hooghly;

(2) Bābu Lalit Mohun Singh, of Sibpur;

(3) Bābu Upendra Nārāyan Nandi, of Shāhāganj.

Of English friends still living I am allowed to reproduce the print of 1877, and its repeat in 1913, of Mr. Frank Courthope, well known in Sussex and in banking circles in London, (next page).

The next is remarkable. Captain V. H. Haggard, R.N., was a child of $2\frac{3}{4}$ years old at Hooghly, 1877. By much ingratiation I succeeded in getting a print of his whole hand, and another of three

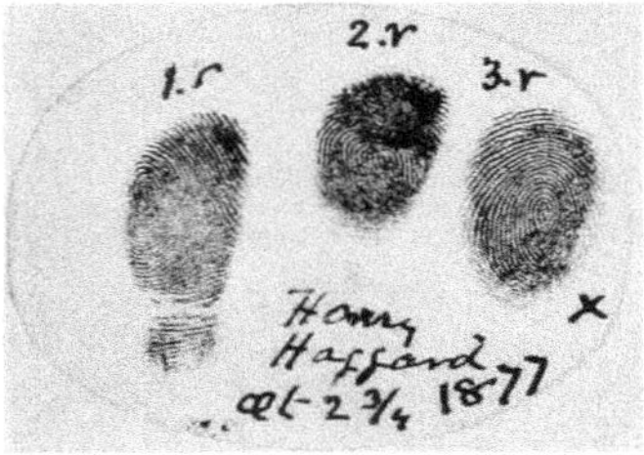

1877 æt. $2\frac{3}{4}$

r 3 1877
(magnified)

Repeat 1913
(magnified)

CAPTAIN V. H. HAGGARD, R.N.

fingers. In 1913, when on special duty in H M.S. 'President', he kindly gave me (not for the first time) a repeat, this time at the age of 38. The baby print bears enlargement beautifully, and I am sure my readers will be delighted with the comparison I am thus able to lay before them.

r. 1 At Hooghly, 1877. | r. 1 r. 2 Oct. 21, 1913. W. F. Courthope. | r. 2 At Hooghly, 1877.

One of the prints I value most, on personal grounds, is that of Sir Theodore Hope, at that time in the Legislative Council of India for Bombay. I grieve to say he has died since these words were written. He was one of my most honoured college friends in the old Haileybury days of 1853.

Among the last prints that I took in India were two at Mussoorie, in the Punjab Himālayas, in Sept. 1877; one of my brother Colonel J. Herschel, R.E., and one of Dr. J. F. Duthie, of the Forest Department. They are both living still, and their repeats to-day are quite good.

To return now to my letter of 1877. I was 'able to say that these marks do not change in the course of ten or fifteen years'. I might have said eighteen years, for my own marks reached back to 1859; but I was steering for safety.

The conviction of the unchanging character of finger-patterns had, of course, grown on me only by degrees, as the evidence of time accumulated. Among my friends, from Nuddea days onwards, I often took second impressions, invariably drawing

r. 1 r. 2

Colonel J. Herschel, Sept. 22, 1877.

r. 1 r. 2

J. F. Duthie, 1877.

attention to their identity with the former ones. I never came upon any sign of change, bar accident. But such comparisons were generally limited to intervals of no more than two or three years, owing to the frequent changes of residence incidental to Indian service. As time went on it was chiefly the incessant evidence of my own ten fingers, and of my whole hand, which wrought in me the overwhelming conviction that the lines on the skin persisted indefinitely.

But besides my own evidence of eighteen years, I had that of my oldest college friend, William Waterfield, of almost as long. On March 31, 1877, he and

Mr. (afterwards Sir Theodore) Hope and Mrs. Hope were my guests at Hooghly. I took all their impressions and my own on that day, noting on Waterfield's that we compared it with his earliest print of

r. 1 r. 2
T. C. Hope, Bo.C.S., at Hooghly, 1877.

r. 1 r. 2
W. Waterfield, July 31, 1860, Nuddea.

r. 1 r. 2
W. Waterfield, March 31, 1877, Hooghly.

1860, in Nuddea, seventeen years earlier. We found the agreement, of course, complete. Here are the facsimiles.

If more evidence were required, I was prepared, without hesitation, to call on any person whose mark I had taken since I began. It was in fact from among those very persons, Natives as well as English, that thirteen years later, at Mr. Galton's request. I obtained the repeats which, by their much longer persistence then, went so far to prove his case to universal conviction.

I close this record with a comparison between three of my own prints, taken, one in 1859, one in

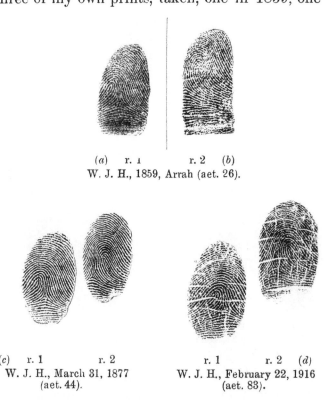

(*a*) r. 1 r. 2 (*b*)
W. J. H., 1859, Arrah (aet. 26).

(*c*) r. 1 r. 2
W. J. H., March 31, 1877
(aet. 44).

r. 1 r. 2 (*d*)
W. J. H., February 22, 1916
(aet. 83).

1877, and the last to-day, after fifty-seven years. For length of persistence they cannot at present be matched.

It goes beyond the proper scope of this narrative, but I cannot refrain from offering my readers here a striking instance of the almost incredible persistency of atomic renovation that takes place in the pads of our fingers, in spite of their being more subject to wear than any other part of the body.

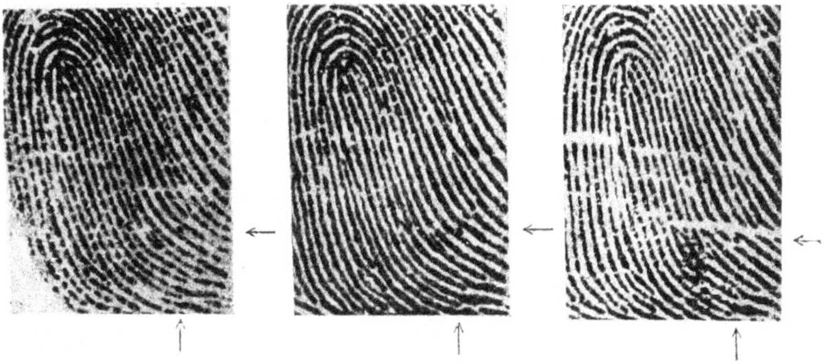

1881, aet. $7\frac{3}{4}$. 1890, aet. 17. 1913, aet. 40.

A. E. H. Herschel, r. 3.

The first was taken at the age of $7\frac{3}{4}$; the next, for Mr. Galton, nine years later. In 1913 my son was in Canada when I asked him to send me several repeats. Every print showed the minute tell-tale dot which Mr. Galton's sharp eye had noticed twenty-two years before. No doubt it was a natal mark. It has anyhow already persisted for thirty-two years.

APPENDIX

When I speak of the 'discovery' of finger-prints nigh sixty years ago, I should wish to be understood correctly. I cannot say that I thought of it as such until Mr. Galton examined old records in search of earlier notices of the subject. What he found had been beyond my ken, and I never inquired for myself. The fascination of experiments and the impelling object of them were all I cared about. Had it been otherwise I should have had an open field for egoism to any extent, for no one questioned the novelty of the thing.

The time that has elapsed since Galton's inquiries, without any material addition to his ascertained facts, justifies me, I venture to think, in speaking of my work as the 'discovery' of the value of finger-prints.

I proceed to show what has been brought to light from other sources.

Bewick.

Of modern cases the first known is that of Thomas Bewick. He was a wood-engraver, as well as an author, and had a fancy for engraving his finger-mark. He printed, as far as I can ascertain, only three specimens, by way of ornament to his books.

1. 1809. 'British Birds', p. 190. The impression of the finger appears as if obliterating a small scene

of a cottage, trees, and a rider, but the paper between the lines of the finger is almost all clean.

2. 1818. The 'Receipt'; of which, by Mr. Quaritch's favour, I possess one. This is, beyond all possibility of doubt, quite free from any tooling. How it was transferred to paper in those days (of which there is an indication) I am unable to say,

but for his purposes it was an original 'finger-print' of Thomas Bewick. Even the fine half-tone process of this facsimile cannot reproduce its delicacy.

3. 1826. Memorial Edition of Bewick's Works, 1885, on the last page of the last volume, under a letter dated 1826, in which he rates some one for copying his woodcuts. When I saw it at the British Museum some years ago I thought it showed tool-work.

These three seem to be all the specimens now available, and they are from three different fingers, of which two are certified to be his own.

Gathering that Mr. Quaritch was exceptionally

familiar with Bewick's life, I told him that I wished to leave no stone unturned to do ample justice to him, if he was known to have done anything more than appears above. Mr. Quaritch took the matter up very kindly, and finally informed me that he had been unable to trace any writing of Bewick's concerning these prints. There seems, therefore, no evidence that he ever took impressions of any finger but his own. Now it is true that no one of observant habits, and least of all an engraver, could fail to perceive the peculiarities of his own finger. The brick-makers of Babylon and Egypt, and every printer since fingers were dirtied by printer's ink, must have noticed them. But it is a long step from that to a study of other men's marks, with a view to identification. What Bewick certainly did do might easily have led him to such a study, but it looks as if he was satisfied with recognizing his own mark.

Remembering, as I have already said, how one of his marks had struck my fancy as a boy, I am disposed to believe that, all unwittingly, I was guided to seize upon a thread which Bewick had let fall.

Purkinje.

Five years after Bewick, Johannes Purkinje, of Breslau, in 1823, read an essay which has been found and examined by Mr. Galton, and partly translated on p. 85 of his 1892 work. Purkinje carried his study of the patterns on fingers beyond all comparison with Bewick's use of them, of whose existence indeed he could hardly have been aware. He worked hard on them for a scientific (medical) purpose. It seemed to me strange that, going so far as he did, he had not hit upon our idea. To satisfy myself I read his work through in 1909. The very last sentence in it seemed to strike a light. Referring to 'the varieties of the tonsils, and especially of the papillae of the tongue, in different individuals' (no mention of fingers), he finishes the sentence and his essay by saying: 'from all which [varieties] sound materials will be furnished for that individual knowledge of the man which is of no less importance than a general knowledge of him is, especially in the practice of medicine.' A fine conclusion indeed, and a stimulating; but no part of his essay conveys an inkling of identification by means of any of the individual varieties on which he always lays stress, not even his pioneer work in the classification of the markings on fingers.

Bengal. The common way for illiterates to sign is to wet the tip of one finger with ink from

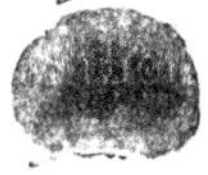

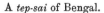

A *tep-sai* of Bengal.

A finger-print.

a pen, and then touch the document (leaving a small black blot) where we touch a wafer. The mark

THE TOKEN-SIGNATURES OF THOSE WHO CANNOT WRITE OR READ, IN SEVERAL CASTES. YEAR 1865. DATE 8 FEBRUARY.

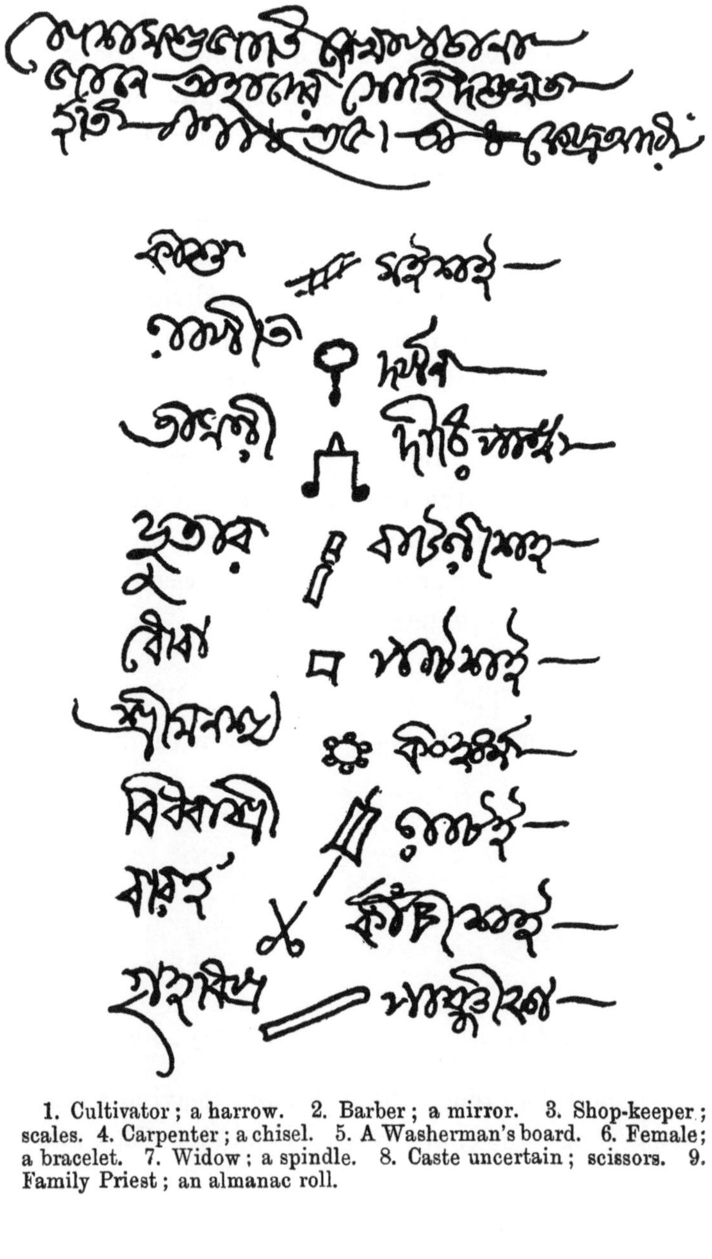

1. Cultivator; a harrow. 2. Barber; a mirror. 3. Shop-keeper; scales. 4. Carpenter; a chisel. 5. A Washerman's board. 6. Female; a bracelet. 7. Widow; a spindle. 8. Caste uncertain; scissors. 9. Family Priest; an almanac roll.

so made is called '*tep-sai*', 'tep' meaning 'pressure' by touch or grip, and 'sai' meaning 'token' (I do not know the etymology). I ask my readers now to compare the '*tep-sai*' with the 'finger-print' alongside it, and to say whether the *tep-sai* could afford any means of identification by comparison with another blot from the same finger. Illiterates who can hold a pen make a cross, as we do, called '*dhera-sai*'; others, more ambitious, indicate their caste by symbols. For the interest of the thing I give some tracings from a collection of such caste-marks which I had made for this purpose when I was Magistrate of Midnapore in 1865.

When I was introducing actual registration I asked the principal member of my Bar to give me his opinion about the new marks. His answer was as follows (the English is of course his own):

Hooghly,
The 21st Aug. /77.

DEAR SIR,

I have examined the impressions made in these papers, and I think each can be distinguished from the others. There are also so many peculiarities in each impression that it cannot be forged, and I think it would be a preventive to forgery if all documents, specially by females, or males who do not know to read or write, would contain impressions by fingers.

Yours faithfully,

ESHAN CHUNDRA MITRA.

I value this letter highly, for Eshan Chundra was

Government Pleader at Hooghly, and in frequent request in Calcutta. No native lawyer of his large practice could have written thus if he had ever known of this method of signature before.

Trustworthy information in my hands is to the effect that attestations by the finger in China are like Bengali *tep-sais*, and nothing more.

China.

The nearest approach to our use of finger-prints that I have found in China came to hand thus:

An Oxford friend, Mr. Bullock, subsequently elected Professor of Chinese, had been interpreter to the Legation in Peking. Talking with him about the methods of signing deeds in China, he told me that the finger-tip (not finger-print) method was in ordinary use, but he was careful to point out also that to his knowledge ever since he went to Peking, about 1868, Chinese bankers had been in the habit of impressing their thumbs on the notes they issued; and he had no doubt the custom was much older than that. This was startling, but he kindly procured for me the bank-note which I here show in facsimile; with it came this explanation of such thumb-marks, given by his friend in China:

'They are imprinted partly on the counterfoil and partly on the note itself, so that when presented its genuineness can be tested at once.'

That is, they play the part of what is technically called the 'scroll' in our cheques.

My readers may accept it that the ink used was

A CHINESE BANK NOTE, 1898

the same Indian ink with which the Chinese characters on the note were written. That is the unhesitating judgement of such an expert as Mr. Galton, who examined it. The difference between a water ink and printer's ink for identification is enormous. Blood on the fingers has occasionally left impressions that fortunately sufficed to reveal the murderer; but, as a rule, wet fingers leave only smudges as useless as this one. It is quite certain, therefore, that no one in the habit of impressing his thumb-mark as this banker did, would use water ink, if he depended on recognizing it as his own. In short, the smudge on the bank-note was placed there in order to identify the two parts of a piece of paper after severance, not to prove who placed it so. My readers may see what exquisite delicacy of detail can be obtained by printer's ink, when so desired, if they will examine a fine skin impression with a magnifying-glass; even the pores along the ridges can be seen as white dots. For practical purposes, however, such extreme delicacy as this is not needed.

This difference of ink suggests a further remark. The Chinese have used printer's ink for ages. If they aimed at identification they would surely have discovered its great value for clear impressions, and its use could never have died out. On the other hand, a method of identification depending on water ink could never have survived for such strict work as our finger-prints. On the palm of the hand it can give a fairly good impression for such simple identification as is wanted (say) for passports, because the large creases will obviously be those of the bearer of the passport, or as obviously not. These lines of the palm, so well known in palmistry, are as clear to a man as the shape of his hand, while those on the pads of his own fingers are scarcely noticed even now by one man in a million. The science of identification by means of the pads cannot, in my opinion, date farther back than 1858, when I happened to use oil-ink, which was not used for *tep-sais*.

The ablest defence of the claims of antiquity that I have seen is by a Japanese writer, Kumagusu Minakata, whose letter to 'Nature', Dec. 27, 1894, appears to be as exhaustive as it is able; but I hope that this paper will satisfy him that the finger-print system of our day has no connexion with the methods he describes. The 'nail-marks' of which he speaks must be utterly useless for identification; yet he treats all manner of impressions alike, and tells us indeed that they are all known by the one name of 'hand-mark'. I fear that he has failed, like some other writers,[1] to see the definite force of the word 'identification' in the finger-print system. It means that if a man can be indicated whose finger-print agrees with that on a document, he is identified with the man who put that one there. That is all we want. But it will be seen that there must be two

[1] I include a too brief notice of the subject by Professor Giles of Cambridge, in his recent work 'Civilization of China', p. 118, and an article in the 'Nineteenth Century' of December 1904.

impressions at least, that will bear comparison, to constitute ‘ identification ’.

None of the writers who have undertaken the defence appears to perceive this need of a second impression if the issue of identity turns on any kind of finger-mark. Repudiations cannot have been rare; tribunals must occasionally have been invoked; yet no instance is quoted of decision by demand for a second impression.

It seems then that these marks were not made, as ours are, expressly to challenge comparison; that, in fact, they offer no points for comparison.

In conclusion, it is hard to believe that a system so practically useful as this could have been known in the great lands of the East for generations past, without arresting the notice of Western statesmen, merchants, travellers, and students. Yet the knowledge never reached us.

FINIS.

For EU product safety concerns, contact us at Calle de José Abascal, 56–1°,
28003 Madrid, Spain or eugpsr@cambridge.org.

www.ingramcontent.com/pod-product-compliance
Ingram Content Group UK Ltd.
Pitfield, Milton Keynes, MK11 3LW, UK
UKHW012342130625
459647UK00009B/481

9781108081252